FRANK

L. FRANK BAUM

ROYAL HISTORIAN OF OZ

Angelica Shirley Carpenter
and Jean Shirley

Lerner Publications Company • Minneapolis

Text permissions, acknowledgments, and source notes appear
on pages 143 and 144, which are an extension of the copyright page.

This book is available in two editions:
Library binding by Lerner Publications Company
Soft cover by First Avenue Editions
241 First Avenue North
Minneapolis, MN 55401

Library of Congress Cataloging-in-Publication Data

Carpenter, Angelica Shirley.
    L. Frank Baum : royal historian of Oz : / Angelica Shirley Carpenter
and Jean Shirley.
      p.   cm.
    Includes bibliographical references and index.
    Summary: A biography of the author of "The Wizard of Oz," who
invented a new kind of fairy tale, uniquely modern and American.
    ISBN 0-8225-4910-7 (lib. bdg.)
    ISBN 0-8225-9617-2 (pbk.)
    1. Baum, L. Frank (Lyman Frank), 1856-1919—Biography—Juvenile
literature. 2. Authors, American—20th century—Biography—Juvenile
literature. 3. Oz (Imaginary place)—Juvenile literature.
[1. Baum, L. Frank (Lyman Frank), 1856-1919. 2. Authors, American.]
I. Shirley, Jean. II. Title.
PS3503.A923Z63   1991
813'.4—dc20   90-27436
[B]   CIP
[92]   AC

Manufactured in the United States of America

2 3 4 5 6 7 8 9 99 98 97 96 95 94 93

Note to Readers

L. Frank Baum was a celebrity in his lifetime and has been the subject of intense study since his death in 1919. Some accounts of his life use fictionalized dialogue, which we have quoted on occasion. All quotations, including all dialogue, in this text come from written sources; see pages 143 and 144.

The sources are books, magazines, newspapers, personal letters, published interviews with the author, and written remembrances of his family and friends. Sometimes these accounts do not agree, but we have tried to describe his life as accurately as possible.

For Frank and his immediate family, we have used the simplest forms of their names, usually the first name.

Frank sometimes varied the way he spelled or capitalized the names of his characters (his editor should have noticed!). We have used one spelling for each character's name throughout this text, except when quoting.

Acknowledgments

Thanks to Robert A. Baum, L. Frank Baum's great-grandson; Michael Gessel, Editor of *The Baum Bugle;* and Barbara S. Koelle, President of the International Wizard of Oz Club, for their help and encouragement.

We also acknowledge our debt to Michael Patrick Hearn, Alla T. Ford, John Fricke, Martin Gardner, David L. Greene, Douglas C. Greene, Peter E. Hanff, Russell P. MacFall, Daniel P. Mannix, Dick Martin, Fred M. Meyer, Raylyn Moore, Russell B. Nye, Frederick E. Otto, Justin Schiller, Jack Snow, Sally Roesch Wagner, and other Baum scholars, whose research made this book possible.

Angelica Shirley Carpenter
Jean Shirley

Contents

Maps appear on pages 30 and 89

In his mid-forties, L. Frank Baum became a successful writer.
These are his first books for children, published from 1897 to 1901.

ONE

Once Upon a Time

1856-1870

On a cold day in Chicago in 1898, Frank Baum, aged 42, buttoned his warm overcoat. He was tall, handsome, and well-dressed, with dark hair, gray eyes, and a full mustache. Frank hated the cold and the fierce wind blowing outside, but he had errands to run and the afternoon was growing late.

As he opened the front door, Frank was rushed by a group of children. "Tell us a story!" they demanded, and they pushed and pulled him back into the cozy house. "A story right away now!"

Four of the boys were his own sons. The children's cheeks were glowing; their noses were running. They stomped off snow and peeled away their wraps. Frank decided his errands could wait.

The children sat around him on the floor. They loved his stories, especially the ones about talking animals. Sometimes Frank's tales continued from one day to the next. This time he told the children a new version of a story they had already heard.

He began with a cyclone, which blew a Kansas farm girl named Dorothy to a magic land. There she met a live Scarecrow, a Tin Woodman, and a Cowardly Lion. Dorothy wanted to go home to Kansas. Her new friends traveled with her to seek advice from the ruler of the land, a powerful Wizard. Their enemy was a Wicked Witch.

As Frank talked, he watched the children's faces. His listeners grew more attentive than ever before. Later he described what happened:

> I was sitting on a hatrack in the hall, telling the kids a story and suddenly this one moved right in and took possession. I shooed the children away and grabbed a piece of paper that was lying there on the rack and began to write. It really seemed to write itself. Then I couldn't find any regular paper, so I took anything at all, even a bunch of old envelopes.

Soon his outline was complete—a stack of papers covered in his left-handed, back-sloping handwriting.

Frank needed a name for his fairyland. Later he said that he was inspired by an unlikely source: his file cabinet. It had three drawers, labeled A-G, H-N, and O-Z. *Oz* was the name he decided to use.

Many different versions of this story have been told, including one by Frank himself in a newspaper interview. But Frank enjoyed making up stories for entertainment or publicity. His wife always insisted that the part about the file cabinet was not true.

What is certain is that Frank's book *The Wonderful Wizard of Oz* became a best-seller in 1900. Today it is still a

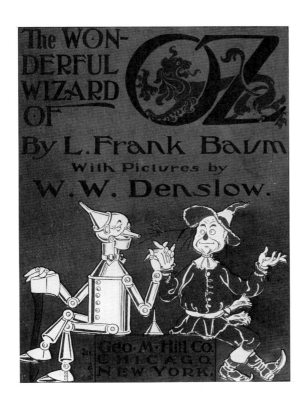

The Tin Woodman and the Scarecrow are known around the world. This is the title page of the first edition.

best-seller. Frank wrote 13 more Oz books, which children still love. But the series is controversial; it has been banned from libraries and schools over the years.

Today the 1939 film *The Wizard of Oz* is better known than the book. It is one of the best movies ever made. And today Frank is the respected author of one of the most famous stories ever written for children. With the Oz series he invented a new kind of fairy tale, uniquely modern and American.

Lyman Frank Baum was born May 15, 1856, in Chittenango, New York, 15 miles (24 kilometers) east of Syracuse. His father's family was German and had come to America in

Cynthia and Benjamin Baum. Some people thought Frank's parents pampered him too much.

1748 seeking religious freedom. Frank's grandfather was a Methodist minister who "rode the circuit" from town to town.

When Frank was born, his father, Benjamin Baum, was a cooper, or manufacturer of barrels. On his land in Chittenango, Benjamin Baum built a house, a barrel factory, and a boardinghouse for factory workers.

When oil was discovered nearby, Benjamin Baum went into the oil business and made a fortune.

Frank's mother was Cynthia Ann Stanton, a devout woman of Scotch-Irish descent. Her family had come to New York from Connecticut. While her husband grew rich, she had baby after baby, and Frank was her seventh child. In those days many children died young. The Baums had nine children in all; two girls and three boys lived to grow up.

Frank was named Lyman after his uncle, but he always preferred the name Frank.

When Frank was about five, his family moved to a 15-acre (6-hectare) farm north of Syracuse, in what is now the Syracuse suburb of Mattydale. Frank's father had a large house built among the rolling green hills. He furnished it in the dark, elaborate style of the 1860s. Winding paths covered with white gravel cut across the lawns like lines on a map. The house was surrounded by fruit trees, grapevines, and hundreds of rose bushes. Cynthia Baum named their new estate Rose Lawn. Even the outhouse was hidden behind a rose trellis.

Frank was a sickly, delicate child. Born with a weak

In this 1901 book by Frank, Dot lives on an estate called Roselawn. With Tot, the gardener's son, she travels to a magic land.

heart, he suffered all his life from angina pectoris. In this condition, the patient's heart receives too little oxygen, especially after meals or exercise. The result is severe chest pains.

Frank's worried parents did not allow him to exert himself. The Baum children did not attend school, but had private tutors at Rose Lawn.

Frank's father owned two neighboring farms where he raised grain, livestock, and chickens. Frank liked to feed the chickens, and sometimes he pretended they could talk.

After he learned to read, he could often be found lying on the floor in his father's library, absorbed in a book. In those days few books were written just for children. Frank read novels, especially those by British authors Charles Dickens and William Makepeace Thackeray. He also enjoyed fairy tales.

Later he remembered, "I demanded fairy stories when I was a youngster... and I was a critical reader too. One thing I never liked then, and that was the introduction of witches and goblins into the story. I didn't like the little dwarfs in the woods bobbing up with their horrors."

Frank decided that someday he would write a new kind of fairy tale for children, with nothing truly frightening.

Sometimes Frank had nightmares, and his parents blamed the fairy tales. One terrifying figure appeared often in his dreams: a scarecrow who came to life and chased him. Later he said, "When I was a boy I was tremendously interested in scarecrows. They always seemed to my childish imagination as just about to wave their arms, straighten up and stalk across the field on their long legs."

The Baums were a loving family whose lives centered around relatives, friends, and church. Mrs. Baum was a strict Episcopalian who believed that Sunday should be devoted to

Frank was a shy boy and spent much time alone in secret places he found. He acted out fantasies, played with imaginary friends, and invented voices for his toys.

God. Her children were forbidden to play croquet or baseball on the Sabbath.

Visiting and entertaining were the family's main social activities. Grown-ups and children played cards and backgammon; they worked puzzles and looked at scenes through a special viewer called a stereoscope. Although Frank was too frail for sledding or hiking, he enjoyed concerts, fireworks, and carriage rides.

When Frank was 12, his doctors found him well enough to go to boarding school. His parents believed he would benefit from military life and discipline.

They enrolled their son in the prestigious Peekskill Academy in Peekskill, New York, 43 miles (69 km) from New York City. The hilltop campus overlooked the beautiful Hudson River.

This high school for boys attracted students from the United States, Japan, and Latin American countries. Peekskill prepared young men for college, civil engineering, business, and United States military academies. It offered a library, laboratory, gymnasium, and student newspaper.

The cadets' military training included competitive drills, shooting, the assault and defense of a fort, athletic games, and boating on the river. The school's goal was to develop "true manly character," gentlemanly conduct, and instant obedience.

Frank hated Peekskill. Classes and marches, homework and church were scheduled for most of each day. Free time and privacy were not important. Frank missed his home and his family.

He never agreed with the military way of thinking. To him, officers were not necessarily superior to privates. He did not like people who considered themselves better than others.

The school rules seemed unreasonably strict, the teachers, demanding and cruel. They slapped the students, or beat them with canes or rulers, even for small offenses.

How Frank finally left Peekskill after two years is unclear. One account says he was punished for looking out the window at birds instead of studying his lesson. Distressed at being punished, he fainted, and some said he suffered a heart attack. Others called his collapse a nervous breakdown.

TWO

A Darned Fool?

1870-1882

Whatever the crisis at Peekskill, Frank's parents relented. They let him return to Rose Lawn, where he continued his studies with a tutor.

Sometimes Frank accompanied Benjamin Baum on business trips to Syracuse. While waiting for his father one day, Frank watched a printing press at work. He was good with machines and began to long for a press of his own.

Small printing presses for home use were popular at this time, costing less than $50. Frank's father bought him a Novelty press, powered by a foot pedal, for his 14th birthday. Soon Frank became skilled at setting type.

With his 11-year-old brother Harry, Frank began a neighborhood newspaper. *The Rose Lawn Home Journal* contained articles, editorials, short stories, poems, and word games. Syracuse stores bought advertisements in the paper, and a lawyer and a veterinarian advertised their services.

Frank (right) *with his wife* (center), *brother Harry, and Harry's wife. The brothers remained close friends all their lives.*

The brothers got their news from books, magazines, and other newspapers. They published verses, like this railroad epitaph:

> Father, mother, sister, me,
> Were run over — here we be.
> The engine was old; the boiler rusted,
> And all of a sudden the darn thing busted!!

Riddles were included:

> Why is an oyster the greatest anomaly in nature? —
> It is a fish without a fin;
> It has a beard without a chin;
> It wears its bones outside its skin;
> And must be out of its bed, to be tucked in.

Frank and Harry also earned money by printing signs, stationery, and programs. In 1873 Frank bought a new printing press and started a new paper, *The Empire*. He also

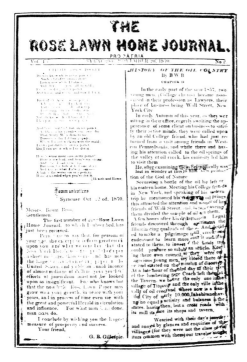
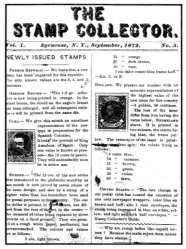

Frank's early publications are valuable to collectors. Very few copies of these papers still exist. This Rose Lawn Home Journal *is from Yale University.*

published a magazine for stamp collectors and became a stamp collector himself.

In his late teens, Frank was tall, confident, and happy with new interests and his family. His health was good enough for camping on Frenchman's Island in Oneida Lake.

Frank had always liked chickens, and in the late 1870s, raising "fancy fowls" (purebred chickens) became a popular fad. Lawyers, businessmen, and wealthy farmers like the Baums took up the hobby. Frank began to breed Hamburgs — small, colorful birds.

With his father and his brother Harry, Frank formed a corporation to breed chickens. The Baums' birds soon won prizes at fairs and exhibitions. Frank organized meetings of poultry associations in several states, and started a new magazine, *The Poultry Record*.

With his father's help, Frank tried a variety of hobbies and jobs. He worked in a relative's store in Syracuse and later as a salesman for his father. After a stint as a reporter in New York City, he opened a print shop in Bradford, Pennsylvania. There he founded the *New Era* newspaper.

As he ended his teens, Frank developed a new interest: the theater. When he went to plays, he studied actors' techniques. He memorized passages from Shakespeare, and then, with money from his father, he formed a Shakespearean troupe. According to one account, "The only successful performance occurred when the ghost of Hamlet's father fell through a hole in the stage. The audience, which happened to be composed of oil workers, was so delighted that the unhappy ghost had to repeat the stunt five times."

Frank, about age 21. A few years later, the mother of the woman he loved called him a "good-for-nothing dreamer."

Frank's father had bought a small chain of opera houses in New York and Pennsylvania. Benjamin Baum made Frank the manager of these theaters, and soon he gave the opera houses to his son.

Frank hired actors who performed a variety of shows. Sometimes he himself acted, under the names George Brooks and Louis F. Baum. Good looks, theatrical presence, and a rich baritone singing voice brought Frank success on the stage. Offstage he was also popular—pleasant company, a charming young man who loved to tell or hear a funny story.

In 1881 Frank wrote a musical, *The Maid of Arran*, a melodrama based on William Black's novel *A Princess of Thule*. Frank changed the setting from Scotland to Ireland and wrote the songs. He was still working on *The Maid of Arran* when he went home for Christmas.

During the holidays, Frank's sister, Harriet Baum Neal, invited him to a party at her house. She wanted him to meet one particular girl. Maud Gage was a sophomore at Cornell University, where she shared a room with Harriet's daughter. Tall and pretty, Maud was known for her independent mind.

Frank was happy to please his sister. The party had already started when he arrived. His aunt Josephine took Maud's arm and led her through the crowded sitting room to Frank, saying:

> "This is my nephew, Frank. Frank, I want you to know Maud Gage. I'm sure you will love her."
>
> "Consider yourself loved, Miss Gage," was [Frank's] smiling acknowledgment of the introduction.
>
> "Thank you, Mr. Baum," she replied as she held out her hand. "That's a promise. Please see that you live up to it."

Maud dressed in the latest fashions—wasp-waisted dresses, tight skirts, and high heels.

Frank soon realized that Maud was the woman for him, but she was not so sure. In January Frank went back to *The Maid of Arran* and Maud returned to Cornell, where she had other male admirers.

Maud Gage had attended a boys' high school in Syracuse. At college her courses included literature, oratory, French, Latin, Anglo-Saxon, geometry, algebra, trigonometry, theory of equations, physiology, entomology, and botany. She took the "woman's" section of "Drill and Military Science," but women did not drill.

Maud's parents lived in Fayetteville, 8 miles (12.8 km) from Syracuse. Her father, Henry Hill Gage, was a prosperous dry-goods merchant. Her mother, Matilda Joslyn Gage, was a nationally known feminist. The Gages had one son and three daughters. Maud was the baby and her mother's favorite child.

The Gages were community leaders. To their cottage on

The Gage parlor, where Frank courted Maud. The cluttered style was popular at this time.

Genesee Street they added the first bay window and bath-room ever seen in Fayetteville. The house was a meeting place for social activists who fought for temperance (the movement that opposed the sale and drinking of alcoholic beverages) and for women's rights.

Matilda Joslyn Gage, Maud's mother, had attended the second Woman's Rights Convention in Syracuse in 1852, before Maud was born. She had taken her small daughter Helen to the conference and had asked to speak. Her moving talk had won her quick acclaim and had helped her to become a national leader in the suffrage movement (the effort to get women the right to vote).

In New York State, laws were more liberal than in other places. Married women could control real estate and the money they earned; they could even sign contracts. But, as in other states, even though they had to pay taxes, they could not vote.

Matilda Gage often raised the issue of taxation without representation. "All the authority you get for taxing women is through the words 'man,' 'he,' 'his' and the like," she wrote. "Oh wise men, can you tell me why 'he' means 'she' when taxes are to be paid and does not mean 'she' when taxes are to be voted upon?"

In her later years Matilda worked with Elizabeth Cady Stanton and Susan B. Anthony. In the upstairs study of the Gage house, the three women wrote a *History of Woman Suffrage*, published in four volumes from 1881 to 1902.

Frank played a wealthy young man on a painting holiday in The Maid of Arran.

Matilda disapproved of Frank Baum as a husband for Maud. He had a reputation for being talented but wasting his abilities. Frequent career changes made him seem unstable, and Matilda doubted he could earn a living on his own.

But *The Maid of Arran*, Frank's play, became a regional hit. Wearing a blond wig, "Louis F. Baum" played a leading role as Hugh Holcomb.

Maud attended the play's Syracuse premiere in the spring of 1882. In June the play opened in New York City, where the *New York Mirror* called Frank's performance "quiet and effective."

During this time Frank visited Maud frequently. He drove to Fayetteville in a black buggy with a high-stepping bay mare borrowed from his father. Frank courted Maud with music, playing the piano and singing. Soon she returned his affection.

When Frank proposed, in the Gages' front parlor, Maud said yes. Then she asked Frank to wait while she told her mother.

Matilda was in the back parlor. Maud closed the sliding doors between the two rooms, but Frank could hear the two women talking. Later he reported what happened:

> I heard Mrs. Gage say: "I won't have my daughter be a darned fool and marry an actor." Maud snapped back: "All right, mother, if you feel that way about it, good bye." "What do you mean, good bye?" Mrs. Gage demanded. "Well," Maud replied, "you just told me I would be a darned fool to marry an actor, and you wouldn't have a daughter of yours do that. I'm going to marry Frank, so, naturally, you don't want a darned fool around the house."

The sheet music from Frank's musical was promoted the same way a soundtrack album from a film is promoted today. Thus, a song could become a hit in the days before recorded music.

THREE

A Land with No Trees

1882-1891

Matilda's laugh broke through the angry words. "All right, Maud," she said. "If you are in love with him and really determined to marry him, you can have your wedding right here at home."

The wedding took place November 9, 1882. Frank and Maud spent their honeymoon at Sarasota Springs, New York, a fashionable resort.

The bridegroom soon resumed his *Maid of Arran* tour, and Maud traveled with the company. They lived in hotels and boardinghouses from Kansas to Ontario to New Jersey.

When Maud became pregnant, Frank resigned from the play and they rented a house in Syracuse. Frank wrote and staged several other unsuccessful plays. During this time he traveled as a salesman for Baum's Castorine, an axle grease. Frank also managed his father's Castorine firm.

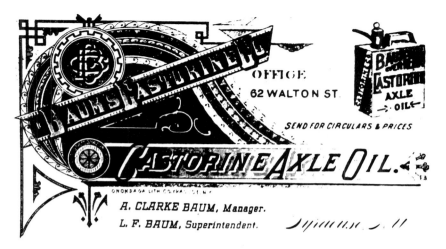

Frank lived in a time when machines were becoming important in everyday life. Oil products powered machines and lubricated their parts.

Maud holds her sons Robert (left) and Frank Jr.

Frank Joslyn Baum (called Frank Jr. in this book) was born in 1883. A second son, Robert Stanton Baum, followed in 1886. After Robert's birth, Maud was seriously ill. For several months she stayed in bed, attended by a nurse. Frank, whose own health was still fragile, made a special effort to amuse the babies. Finally Maud recovered.

Frank let his wife have the upper hand at home. She insisted on controlling their personal finances, as Frank was never good at managing money.

To Please a Child, the biography of Frank written by Russell P. MacFall and Frank Jr., tells the family story known as "the affair of the Bismarks."

Frank bought a dozen filled doughnuts, called bismarks, and took them home for breakfast the next day. Maud demanded to know if he was unhappy with the food *she* bought. Frank said no, he just liked bismarks, too.

He ate two the first morning, two the second. On the third day, he declared the bismarks too stale to eat, but Maud served them again on day four.

Frank wrapped them in a newspaper and hid them in a cupboard.

Maud served them again the next morning, saying, "It seems as if we are playing games, doesn't it?"

That day Frank buried them, but Maud dug them up and washed off the dirt. She served them again next morning.

"For Heaven's sake, Maud," said Frank, "let's stop this nonsense. Those things are not fit to eat and you know it."

"You bought them without consulting me," she replied, "so you will have to eat them. I am not going to have food wasted. But I'll let you off this time if you will promise never again to buy any food unless I ask you to get it."

Frank's interest in raising chickens produced his first

book. In 1886 *The Book of the Hamburgs* was published by a small Connecticut publisher.

Frank's father died in 1887 when Frank was 31. Benjamin Baum had lost most of his fortune by then—the commercial farms and even Rose Lawn. Frank continued with the Castorine business.

One morning when he went to the office, he made a grisly discovery: the company clerk, shot dead, lying across a desk. The man had committed suicide after gambling away the firm's money. Frank had to sell the Castorine business, and his opera houses also failed.

"Western fever" was the talk of the nation. In Dakota Territory, it started with the discovery of gold in the 1870s. Miners flocked to the Black Hills, despite an 1868 treaty promising that Native Americans could keep this land forever.

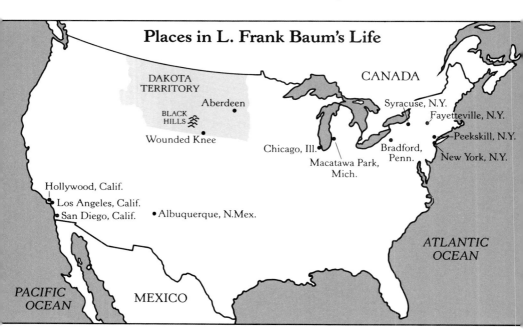

Places in L. Frank Baum's Life

Settlers, including Maud's brother Clarkson, her two sisters, and many others from Syracuse, soon followed and founded towns throughout the territory. They settled in Aberdeen, a new town built where two railroad lines crossed. The government gave free land to homesteaders.

Clarkson wrote of rich soil and good conditions for farming. There were no trees to cut down, he explained, just windy plains to plow. He had made his money from grain. He wrote that sales were in cash, that a storekeeper could make a living selling needed goods to miners and farmers.

In April 1886, Clarkson wrote to describe his new daughter: "We have a 'fine jinks' of a baby at our house by the name of Matilda Jewell Gage."

Frank replied:

> You will now begin to enjoy the felicity of living in earnest. You can awaken a dozen or two times each night and sooth [sic] your daughter. You can trot her all your evenings upon your knee... You can walk the floor with her over your shoulder, and have a friend point out to you when you reach the store a streak of milky substance down the back of your best coat... Let us... cling only to thoughts of the sweet, innocent child faces that will brighten our lives for years to come, and make us thank God heartily that they arrived at all.
>
> Ever thine,
> L. F. Baum.

Frank visited Aberdeen in June 1888. The *Aberdeen Daily News* reported, "L. Frank Baum of Syracuse, New York, who has been visiting his in-laws here finds recreation from the cares of an extensive business in the fascinating pursuit, amateur photography. Mr. Baum is proficient in the art and during his stay in the city secured a number of fine negatives of Dakota land and cloud scapes."

Frank developed and printed the pictures himself. He liked Aberdeen, and in September he moved there with Maud, four-year-old Frank Jr., and two-year-old Robert.

Aberdeen had 3,000 residents, many young and well educated. Later Clarkson's daughter, the "fine jinks of a baby," Matilda Jewell Gage, described the town as it looked when the Baums arrived.

> The Main Street of Aberdeen...was crowded for several blocks with live stores shops [sic], hotels, brick buildings and two very handsome stone front bank edifices. To these can be added two depots and freight offices, a U.S. Land Office, three large [grain] elevators, two school buildings, four churches and other structures. As the streets were not yet paved, the sidewalks of wooden planks were raised above the level of the roads. Since 1886 there had been electric service and the water supply came from artesian wells. Gas was used for lighting.

The Baums rented a house and, from Maud's sister Helen and her husband, they rented a store.

Baum's Bazaar opened on October 1, 1888. The store offered a wide assortment of tableware, glassware, lamps, baskets, toys, candy, and novelties.

The Bazaar showed no profit at first, but Frank and Maud were not discouraged. They found a congenial social life in Aberdeen. Frank helped organize a bicycle club, performed in amateur theatricals, and managed a prize-winning baseball team. There were musicales, dances, and card parties, and the Baums joined an Equal Suffrage Club.

Above: *Matilda Jewell Gage the "fine jinks" of a baby, is one of two little girls seated at right, beside the building that held Baum's Bazaar. Below: Frank acted with this amateur theater group in Aberdeen.*

Sometimes they entertained friends with séances. Sitting around a table, holding hands in the dark, they tried to contact the dead. Maud claimed that the table tipped and that sometimes they heard a knock.

In the fall of 1888, a group of Sioux leaders rode into town on their way to Washington, D.C. Sitting Bull and the other chiefs were on a peaceful mission, but they were angry that the government had violated the treaty of 1868. President Grover Cleveland had summoned the men. He wanted to buy their land as a way of getting around the treaty. By this time, the United States government had decided that all Native Americans should live on reservations.

In Aberdeen the townspeople worried more about crops than they did about the Indians. The year 1888 ended in a terrible drought, and 1889 was no better. Frank's customers grew poorer.

In the 1880s, Sitting Bull toured with Buffalo Bill Cody and his Wild West show. He hoped that good publicity from his appearances would help his people.

Maud's niece Matilda said that in 1889, it was "109° in the shade on July 2nd with a strong wind blowing the dust." People knew that the wheat crop would fail for a second year.

In November 1889, South Dakota became a state. By this time many businesses had failed, and Baum's Bazaar was nearly bankrupt. Farmers could not earn money if they could not sell wheat. Frank found it impossible to deny his friends and neighbors what they needed, and 161 customers owed him money.

Maud encouraged Frank through the hard times. Their third son, Harry Neal Baum, was born December 17, 1889. Frank loved all children, and they loved him. Sometimes he ignored his customers in the store and sat outside on the wooden sidewalk, telling stories to a group of children.

In January 1890, the bank foreclosed on Baum's Bazaar. But Frank soon found a new job running a weekly newspaper, *The Aberdeen Saturday Pioneer*. He bought some illustrations and articles from a news service and wrote the rest of the paper himself. He sold advertisements, set the type, and ran the printing press.

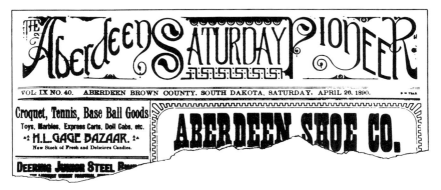

With Frank as editor, The Aberdeen Saturday Pioneer *became known for its wit and its attractive layout.*

The column called "Our Landlady" was the paper's most popular feature. "Mrs. Bilkins" owns a boardinghouse where she discusses timely subjects with her boarders. Her speech, written in dialect, shows her to be uneducated.

In one column the landlady describes her visit to a farm, where she sees an unusual wagon. "I rubbed my eyes in amazement for a minit," she tells her boarders, "cause there was no hoss or beast o' any kind hitched to it." The wagon is powered by electricity, she explains, and machines perform all the work on the farm. They cook dinner, set the table, and wash the dishes—amazing ideas to Frank's readers.

In another column, Mrs. Bilkins tells of a farmer putting green goggles on his cattle. Then the animals eat wood shavings, believing they are grass. Mrs. Bilkins describes an enormous book, called *Baum's Hourly Newspaper,* which contains all world events of the past hour.

The *Pioneer* covered Aberdeen social events. One wedding story got Frank into trouble. The angry bridegroom arrived at the newspaper office, determined to horsewhip the editor. Frank had described the bride as having a "roguish smile," but a typographical error changed the word to "roughish." Ladies were not supposed to be rough. Some "loungers" at the newspaper office talked the furious reader into solving the problem by fighting a duel. One man sent home for his dueling pistols. Soon Frank and his opponent, guns in hand, stood back to back in the street.

The plan called for them to walk around the block in opposite directions until they met behind the newspaper office. Either man could fire at any point, but Frank did not shoot. Instead, as he turned the corner, he ran. Hearing footsteps behind him, he ran faster.

Then one of his friends caught up with him and said,

"Come back, Frank. Your opponent ran off in the other direction."

"[Frank] returned to the scene and, brandishing his pistol, shouted, 'Where is that coward? Lead me to him!'"

In his paper Frank advocated votes for women. He called women activists *suffragists.* Feminist leaders preferred this name to the more common (and belittling) term, *suffragettes.*

The *Pioneer* covered wars, politics, and plans for the World Columbian Exposition in Chicago. It reported train wrecks, raids on opium dens, and murders by "White Caps" (the Ku Klux Klan).

Local stories discussed seed wheat for needy farmers, the fight over where to locate the state capital, and a cyclone that hit Aberdeen in May 1890.

Later that year the paper told of the last chapter in the struggle now known as the Indian Wars. Wovoka, a young leader from the Paiute tribe in Nevada, had visions in which white settlers were driven from Native American lands. His followers danced a "ghost dance," which spread to all the western tribes. In several states, large groups of Native Americans gathered to dance. This great movement made settlers uneasy, even in peaceful areas like Aberdeen.

Government officials claimed that Indians had been spoiled by government handouts. On December 13, the *Pioneer* quoted Senator Sanders of Montana, who had written, "Every consideration has been shown the savages... [W]e ourselves have determined that the continent belongs to civilization as a matter of morals, and we have further determined that we are civilization... We are making extraordinary endeavors to have the copper-hued loafer work for his living."

Meanwhile Sioux gathered in central South Dakota. The

government did not want Sitting Bull, a powerful leader, to join the ghost dance movement. The army sent Native American police to arrest him (some said to murder him) at his village on the Grand River.

"HIS LAST FIGHT," read the *Pioneer's* headline on December 27. In the story, an Indian Agent tells how Sitting Bull was dragged forcibly from his house. A struggle broke out between Indian police and Sitting Bull's followers, and Sitting Bull was shot dead.

The great chief's followers fled, and some turned to another leader, Big Foot. They were soon defeated in the terrible slaughter at Wounded Knee Creek. About 300 Native Americans—men, women, and children—died in this last battle of the Indian Wars.

Burying the dead after the Battle of Wounded Knee, S.D.-1890.

The U.S. army hired civilians to bury the dead at Wounded Knee. Pay was two dollars a body.

Frank's younger sons, Kenneth (left) *and Harry, in their best clothes. Frank had a trunk full of costumes and wigs, which the boys used for dress-up and play-acting.*

In Aberdeen, daily life continued normally. Frank Jr. started school. A fourth son, Kenneth Gage Baum, was born in March 1891. The next month Frank lost the newspaper to bankruptcy, or, as he said, "I decided the sheriff wanted the paper more than I did."

Above: *Maud with* (from left) *Robert, Harry, Kenneth, and Frank Jr., in 1900.* Below: *The living room of the Baums' Humboldt Park home in Chicago.* From left, *Frank Jr., Robert, Harry (petting the cat), Kenneth, and Frank.*

FOUR

The Windy City

1891-1899

In Chicago, plans were under way for a world's fair. Several cities had competed to host the event, with New York and Chicago the main contenders. Richard Henry Dana of the New York *Sun* claimed that Chicago boosters produced a lot of "hot air," so he nicknamed the town "the Windy City."

In 1890 the United States Congress awarded the fair to Chicago. On the shore of Lake Michigan, workers dug canals and lagoons, and built white palaces. The fair attracted many artists and writers to Chicago, among them Frank.

He arrived in May 1891 and found a job reporting for the *Evening Post*. Maud soon followed with Frank Jr., aged seven; Robert, aged five; Harry, one-and-a-half; and Kenneth, just five months old.

Frank had rented a house on the West Side, at 34 Campbell Park, without a bathroom or running water. Because

Frank's salary was only $20 per week, Maud helped by teaching young women to embroider for 10 cents a lesson.

After the newspaper cut Frank's salary to $18.62 a week, he found a new job as buyer of crockery for a department store. Soon he became a traveling salesman for a china company, Pitkin and Brooks. Later his son Harry recalled that, "because he had no idea of what his sales should be, he secured orders for an amazing volume and became almost overnight the firm's leading salesman."

Maud's mother often visited. Grandmother Gage, as the family now called Matilda, kept Maud company when Frank was on the road.

Frank taught his customers to arrange displays with the china they bought, and to spruce up their stores. His son Harry recalled Frank's idea for the window of a hardware store. He revolted against merely stacking item on item, according to Harry:

> He wanted to create something eye-catching, so he made a torso out of a washboiler, bolted stovepipe arms and legs to it, and used the underside of a saucepan for the face. He topped it with a funnel hat, and what would become the inspiration for the tin woodman [sic] was born.

The Baums, and all Chicago, were delighted when the World Columbian Exposition finally opened in May 1893. It celebrated the 400th anniversary of Columbus's discovery of America. New machines and elaborate effects with electric lights predicted life in the coming century—the 1900s.

The fair was nicknamed The White City. Its 200 enormous buildings glowed like marble in the sun. The ornate architecture included domes, arches, and columns.

Inside were "cannibals," steam engines, and exotic fish in an aquarium. Fairgoers could see Egyptian dancers, Pullman train cars, and the latest five-color printing presses. Thomas Edison's newest invention, the Kinetoscope, showed moving pictures.

One morning Maud took Frank Jr. and Robert, the two older boys, to the fair. They planned to meet Frank for lunch at the Woman's Building.

Frank and Maud did not know that on this particular day a luncheon was scheduled for that building. Eulalia, the Infanta (daughter of the monarch) of Spain, was guest of honor.

When Frank arrived, a huge crowd had gathered. He could not get into the building, and he could not see Maud and the boys anywhere.

To get through the crush, he joined a procession marching into the hall. Frank, always well dressed, fit in with the other men in the group. Soon he found himself at a banquet table, being served a fine lunch. His son Harry said later:

> Making the best of the situation, he was enjoying himself among his companions when some compelling force drew his attention to the balcony surrounding the reception area. And there, pressed tightly against the rail with a small child clutching either hand, was a tired and hungry mother staring at him in amazement and anger!

Maud's temper was famous. On another occasion, Frank Jr. reported:

> We had a cat and due to some childish perversity I took it upstairs one day and threw it out the second story window. Fortunately the cat wasn't hurt, but

my mother saw me do it and to teach me a lesson, caught me up and held me out the window pretending that she was going to drop me. But it was quite real to me and I screamed so loudly that the neighbors all rushed out and were quite horrified by the spectacle of my mother dangling me out of the window, not sure but she would let me drop. Needless to say, I was quite cured of throwing cats out of windows.

Frank let Maud handle the discipline because he hated to punish the boys. Once he spanked Kenneth, but he felt so guilty that later he woke his son to apologize to him.

By 1895 Frank was earning enough to move the family one block, to a nicer house with indoor plumbing.

Frank's mother visited occasionally. Even to his mother, Frank told fantastic stories as if they were true. He started with ordinary facts and then added amazing details. One such tale fooled his mother for a time.

When she realized what was happening, she said, "Frank, you are telling me a story."

He answered quickly, "Well, Mother, as you know, St. Paul in his Epistle to the Ephesians said 'All men are liars.'"

His mother thought for a moment, but she could not recall the verse. She took out her Bible to check, only to realize he had fooled her again.

Sometimes Frank was away for weeks at a time. He wrote Maud every day.

Maud's mother began to spend winters with them. She still did not approve of her son-in-law. Matilda wrote to Maud's sister, "L. F. comes in Friday. He failed to receive M's letter for a day or two and telegraphed her—seems he wouldn't travel if he didn't hear, &c &c—a perfect baby."

Matilda Joslyn Gage (left) *predicted Frank would never have enough money to keep the wolf from the door. Cynthia Baum* (right) *disapproved when her grown-up son attended baseball games on the Sabbath.*

But even Matilda Joslyn Gage admired Frank's story-telling. In the evenings after supper, neighborhood children gathered at the Baum home to listen to Frank. On cold nights they popped corn and pulled taffy; in summer they cranked an ice-cream freezer. Each night at nine, the policeman on the beat rang the doorbell, then watched the visitors safely home.

Often Frank read the children Mother Goose rhymes. Harry and Kenneth could not understand some of the verses. Why, they demanded, did the mouse run up the clock? How could blackbirds survive being baked in a pie? How could a cow jump over the moon?

Matilda urged Frank to write down his explanations, to send them to a publisher of children's books. Frank could not believe anyone would want his stories, but Maud said firmly, "Mother is nearly always right about everything."

In Mother Goose in Prose, *Humpty Dumpty leaves his mother's nest when his brother eggs roll around and kick him.*

Frank was a member of the Chicago Press Club. There he met Chauncey L. Williams of Way & Williams publishers. In 1897 this firm published Frank's *Mother Goose in Prose*, with illustrations by Maxfield Parrish, a promising young artist from Philadelphia. *Mother Goose* was Parrish's first book, too, the first major success of his famous career.

Frank autographed Maud's copy of the book, "One critic I always fear and long to please. It is my Sweetheart . . . What does my sweetheart, my wife of fifteen years, think of it?"

Frank's mother-in-law died in 1898. She had lived long enough to see modest sales for *Mother Goose in Prose*. Money from the book helped. Frank suffered severe chest pains, and a heart specialist advised him to quit traveling and take a less demanding job.

Frank started a monthly journal to help store owners. *The Show Window* succeeded, and in 1900 Frank published a book, *The Art of Decorating Dry Goods Windows and Interiors*.

Frank wrote his book *By the Candelabra's Glare* as a gift for friends and relatives. This thin book of poems was made entirely by hand. Frank set the type and printed 99 copies on a foot-powered press in his basement workshop.

In the introduction he states, "My best friends have never called me a poet . . . and I have been forced to admire their restraint."

Artist William Wallace Denslow, another friend from the Chicago Press Club, contributed two pictures to this book. Denslow was tall and dark, with a huge mustache. His posters had won him international fame. Denslow was known to his friends as Hippocampus Den. *Hippocampus* means *seahorse*. Denslow's trademark signature included a seahorse.

Like Frank, Denslow had been drawn to Chicago by the world's fair. The Chicago *Herald* paid him $70 a week to draw pictures of the fair for the newspaper.

As a traveling salesman, Frank had amused himself by writing poems on envelopes and scraps of paper. He had saved these efforts, which resembled Mother Goose rhymes. Now he showed the verses to Denslow, who agreed to illustrate them for a children's book.

This book would change the way children's books were published.

Cover for Father Goose, His Book. *"Nothing could be more delicious,"* said one critic, *"than the expression on Old Father Goose's face as he 'takes his pen in hand' to write down his merry ditties. Even the goose laughs."*

FIVE

Father Goose

1899-1900

Frank typed his poems himself. He was a fast typist though he used only two fingers. Denslow visited frequently to consult about illustrations. Frank's son Harry wrote later:

> I recall that "Den" as we called him, had a striking red vest of which he was inordinately fond. And whenever he came to our house, he would always complain of the heat as an excuse to take off his coat and spend the evening displaying his beautiful red vest. The family used to joke about it among ourselves, but it was a touchy subject with Denslow and we were careful not to say anything about this vanity during his visits.

The book of poems was hard to sell because of a radical idea: Frank and Denslow wanted color on each page. In those days illustrations were usually black and white. Color printing raised the price of a book, and lowered the publisher's profits.

William Wallace Denslow was the same age as Frank. He was known for his corncob pipe, his foghorn voice, and a contrary sense of humor.

Finally Frank and Denslow found a publisher, George M. Hill. Author and artist shared the cost of production with the Hill Company.

Father Goose, His Book appeared in September 1899, just in time for the Christmas trade. Critics loved the book, but some reviewers thought Denslow's pictures outshone Frank's verses. One critic said it was "almost ablaze with color when compared to the usual children's book of the day."

Father Goose sold 75,000 copies the first year, making it the best-selling children's book of 1899. Frank and Denslow split royalties (payment for each book sold).

FATHER GOOSE

Old Mother Goose became
quite new,
And joined a Woman's Club;
She left poor Father Goose
at home
To care for Sis and Bub.

They called for stories by the score,
And laughed and cried to hear
All of the queer and merry songs
That in this book appear.

When Mother Goose at last returned
For her there was no use;
The goslings much preferred to hear
The tales of FATHER GOOSE.

To save typesetting costs, Denslow hired artist Ralph Fletcher Seymour to hand-letter the pages of Father Goose. *Reviewers praised the large print as attractive and easy for children to read.*

Christmas 1899, and all Christmases were happy for the Baums. Son Harry said later:

> WE ALWAYS had a Christmas tree, and this was purchased by Father and set up in the front parlor behind drapes that shut off the room. This, Father explained, was done to help Santa Claus, who was a very busy man, and had a good many houses with children to call upon.
>
> Santa Claus (Father) came a little later to deck the tree, and we children heard him talking to us behind the curtains. We tried to peek through cracks in the curtains, but although we could hear Santa Claus talking, we never managed to see him, and only heard his voice.

Frank gave this photo of himself to Maud. On the back he wrote,
"To my own Sweet Love. The image of your baby. Tooken [sic]
December 1899." Right: *Maud in 1900.*

On Christmas Day, when the curtains were
opened, there was the Christmas tree that Santa
Claus had decorated—a blaze of different colors, and
the presents for each of the boys stacked below it!

"One Christmas," Harry said, "we had *four* Christmas
trees—one for each of the four boys—in the four corners of
the room!"

When summer came, the Baums rented a cottage at a
Michigan resort town, Macatawa Park. Frank named the cottage The Hyperudenbuttscoff. He painted the name on a
sign and hung it outside.

Passersby stopped often, trying to pronounce the
strange word and wondering what it meant. Frank got the
name from a Chicago museum exhibit. The word referred to

a whale's skeleton, but the Baums used it to mean anything hard to describe.

Macatawa Park was on a channel connecting Lake Michigan to the 6-mile-long (9.6-km-long) Lake Macatawa. Frank, who still edited *The Show Window*, commuted to Chicago by boat. He went home to Macatawa on weekends. The Saturday 2:00 P.M. boat from Chicago got him home in time for supper at 7:30.

The Baums found new friends in Michigan. Maud started card clubs, and Frank organized a water carnival, decorating boats and buildings with Japanese lanterns. There were sailing races and dances at the Yacht Club, where Frank started an amateur night, or talent show. Many evenings ended at the Baums', with Frank cooking for the crowd.

Frank smoked cigars, though he knew they were bad for his health. Often he held an unlit cigar in his mouth. One friend said he chewed up about six cigars a day.

When someone asked why he did not light his cigar, Frank insisted that he did, but only when he went swimming. "'You see,' he explained gravely, 'I can't swim, so when the cigar goes out I know I'm getting over my depth.'"

Frank wrote a book about Macatawa, which he called *Tamawaca Folks, A Summer Comedy*. It was published privately and sold in Macatawa stores. The author's name was given as John Estes Cooke, but Frank's neighbors knew who wrote it.

After *Father Goose* was published, the Baums moved to a new home in Chicago at 68 Humboldt Park Boulevard. At Macatawa, Frank bought a larger cottage.

He named the new cottage The Sign of the Goose, honoring the book that had paid for it. Frank suffered at this time from an attack of facial paralysis. Maud explained later:

Above: *The Sign of the Goose cottage* (center, with stairs to shore) *at Macatawa Park, Michigan, 1905.* Below: *Frank painted green geese flying around the living room walls at The Sign of the Goose. He painted over stencils, or cut-out patterns, to make this frieze design.*

His doctor told him to stop writing and do some manual work, so he made a whole set of furniture for our living room—rocker, arm and straight chairs, table, stools and couch—all had leather seats put on with brass strips. Also had a stained glass window with a goose on it . . . On the front porch was a rocking chair, the two sides of which were big geese.

The boys were growing up. Frank Jr., who wanted a military career, applied for admission to Annapolis and West Point. Robert, known as Rob, experimented with electricity. Frank wrote to his brother Harry, now a doctor, "Rob fills the house with electric batteries . . . and we are prepared to hear a bell ring whenever we open a door or step on a stair."

At the dinner table, Maud always tucked her legs under her chair so the boys could not accidentally kick her during debates. Harry said, "To settle the frequent points of dispute which arose, a small shelf was built in the dining room where a dictionary, a single-volumed encyclopedia, and an atlas were kept for quick, convenient reference and decision."

Frank still loved puns, such as this one from *Father Goose*:

Now once I owned a funny man,
A clockwork was inside him;
You'd be surprised how fast he ran
When I was there beside him.
He was the pride of all the boys
Who lived within our town;
But when this man ran up a hill
He always would run down.

Harry said, "When Father made an especially far-fetched pun, we would all laugh uproariously and then reach out our hands to him for any loose change as a reward for laughing."

Soon Frank and Denslow began work on their second major book. At first they called it *The Emerald City*, until they learned of a publishing superstition: any book with a jewel in the title is bound to fail. So they changed the name to *The Wonderful Wizard of Oz*. For this book, they again insisted on colored illustrations.

George M. Hill refused to publish it, as did every other publisher in Chicago, claiming color was too expensive. The publishers objected to the subject matter as well. In those days, books for children were supposed to be educational and uplifting. This was just a fairy tale—plenty of those old-fashioned stories were already in print.

Finally Hill took a chance, publishing the book in the fall of 1900. It sold for $1.50.

The Wonderful Wizard of Oz contained more than 100 illustrations with 24 color plates. The color of the pictures matched Oz geography, with blue illustrations for the chapters set in the Munchkin Country, green for the Emerald City, and so on.

In the book's introduction, Frank said:

> The time has come for a series of newer "wonder tales" in which the stereotyped genie, dwarf and fairy are eliminated, together with all the horrible and blood-curdling incident devised by their authors to point a fearsome moral to each tale.
> ..."The Wonderful Wizard of Oz" was written solely to pleasure children of to-day. It aspires to being a modernized fairy tale, in which the wonderment and joy are retained and the heart-aches and nightmares are left out.

The Lion has just bounded from the forest, hit the Scarecrow, knocked the Tin Woodman to the ground, and tried to bite Toto. Dorothy has slapped the Lion on the nose.

In fact, Frank's story built on the tradition of fantasy adventures. A cyclone carries Dorothy and her dog, Toto, from her Aunt Em and Uncle Henry to the land of the Munchkins, in the fairyland of Oz. Oz, she learns, is surrounded by an uncrossable desert, but Dorothy struggles bravely to get back to Kansas.

At the start of her quest, Dorothy receives silver shoes and a magic kiss from the good Witch of the North. Then she walks across Oz on the yellow brick road. Frank improved on the tradition of the kind friend who helps the heroine. He created the Scarecrow, the Tin Woodman, and the Cowardly Lion. But when Dorothy gets to the Emerald City, she faces the Wizard all alone.

The Wizard will help her, he says, if she kills the Wicked Witch of the West. Frank may have deplored "horrible and blood-curdling incidents," but he knew a scary plot and wicked villains kept readers interested.

By the time Dorothy gets back to Kansas, she has learned that things are not always as they appear to be, and that she has the power within herself to achieve her goals.

Artist Denslow portrayed Dorothy as a chunky farm girl about seven years old, with long brown hair in thick braids.

Frank, the writer, made her practical. She melts the Witch with a pail of water:

> The Witch fell down in a brown, melted, shapeless mass and began to spread over the clean boards of the kitchen floor. Seeing that she had really melted away to nothing, Dorothy drew another bucket of water and threw it over the mess. She then swept it all out the door.

"I have been wicked in my day, but I never thought a little girl like you would ever be able to melt me and my wicked deeds. Look out— here I go!" cried the Witch.

Critics liked the book. The *New York Times* wrote: "It will indeed be strange if there be a normal child who will not enjoy the story." Many reviewers compared *The Wizard* to *Alice's Adventures in Wonderland*, the classic fantasy by Lewis Carroll. For a second time, some critics judged Denslow's art to be a greater achievement than Frank's writing. *The Wonderful Wizard of Oz* became the best-selling children's book of 1900.

At first Frank did not realize how well the book was doing. When Maud needed Christmas money, she told Frank to ask his publisher for an advance. This meant payment for books that would be sold later. Frank preferred to wait for his regular payment, but he hated to disappoint the boys. Finally he agreed to ask for $100.

He called on George Hill at the publisher's office. When Hill heard what Frank wanted, he summoned his bookkeeper. Hill told the man to write out a check for all the money the firm owed Frank. Frank pocketed the check without looking at it.

When he got home, Maud was ironing his other shirt. Frank gave her the check—made out for $3,432.64! Maud was so excited that she burned a hole in his shirt.

Above: *David Montgomery as the Tin Woodman and Fred Stone as the Scarecrow in the stage show* The Wizard of Oz. *Stone held perfectly still for the first 18 minutes he was on stage, and then came to life.* Below: *This poster advertises the extravaganza.*

SIX

Extravaganza!
1901-1903

In 1901 Frank and Denslow worked together on a stage show, but first they published the book *Dot and Tot of Merryland*. In this fantasy adventure, two children meet the Queen of Merryland, a large wax doll. Although Frank praised Denslow's *Dot and Tot* illustrations, by the end of 1901 he was on bad terms with the gruff artist.

After *The Wonderful Wizard of Oz*, Denslow worked on his own for a time. He wrote and illustrated *Denslow's Mother Goose*, a great success. Then he published a "Father Goose" comic page in several newspapers.

Frank was outraged because he considered the *Father Goose* characters to be his invention. Despite their differences, writer and artist soon began work on a stage show, with composer Paul Tietjens. Tietjens, who was 23, wanted to write a comic opera. He would write the music, Frank

From top, *Paul Tietjens, W. W. Denslow, (in self-portrait with the scarecrow),and L. Frank Baum. Frank and Tietjens argued that Denslow didn't deserve a third of the profits for the show, but they gave in to him when he threatened to sue them.*

would write the script and song lyrics, and Denslow would design the costumes.

Denslow thought they should prepare a stage version of *The Wonderful Wizard of Oz*, but Frank wrote a musical called *The Octopus*. This title referred to political business scandals. By May 1901 Frank and Tietjens were performing their songs for theater managers, who showed no interest.

Finally the trio gave up on *The Octopus*, and Frank wrote a musical based on *The Wonderful Wizard of Oz*. Frank's son Robert recalled later how the three men worked together at the Baum home.

> I can remember the three of them cutting up like a bunch of school boys. Tejens [sic] would pound out a piece on the piano and father would sing the words or perhaps do a tap or eccentric dance, accompanied by the ferocious Denslow, who was a thick set man with a heavy "walrus" mustache and looked like a brigand. It was better than a vaudeville show to us boys.

Frank and Tietjens took the show to Fred Hamlin, business manager of Chicago's Grand Opera House. Hamlin liked the show because of the word *wizard* in the title. His father, who owned the theater, had earned a fortune selling Hamlin's Wizard Oil, a patent medicine. The younger Hamlin thought his father would enjoy seeing the word *wizard* in lights on the theater marquee.

Hamlin recruited Julian Mitchell, a successful New York stage director. On Mitchell's advice, Frank hired two experts to help him rewrite the musical as an extravaganza. This kind of show contains comedy routines, popular songs, and striking visual effects. Often these acts have nothing to do with the plot. Thus the songs Tietjens wrote for *The Octopus* could be used in *The Wizard of Oz*. "When You Love, Love, Love" became the show's biggest hit.

Frank rewrote his script following Julian Mitchell's directions, even though he disapproved of the changes. For the play, Dorothy became a young woman rather than a little girl. This change allowed her a romance with a newly created character, Dashemoff Daily, the poet laureate of Oz.

Mitchell cast *The Wizard of Oz* with players from vaudeville, a popular kind of show with singing, dancing, and comedy acts. Anna Laughlin, a major star, played Dorothy. The part of the poet was played by a woman, Bessie Wynn, dressed as a man. This part was known as the "trouser role" in British theatrical tradition. The trouser role actress always dressed as a woman in the play's final scene.

The little dog Toto was changed to a cow named Imogene, played by Edwin Stone. Arthur Hill, a British actor, played the Cowardly Lion. His costume weighed 80 pounds (36 kilograms).

Director Mitchell sent for Montgomery and Stone, a rising pair of comedians. David Montgomery played the Tin Woodman. In vaudeville he was known as "the patter man," who did most of the talking. Fred Stone played the Scarecrow. The role seemed perfect for his famous funny walk, almost on his ankles.

The show opened June 16, 1902, to a packed house. Frank, dressed in a business suit, sat with Maud in a box. He was nervous but tried not to show it. Two of the boys sat in another part of the theater.

A member of the audience, Max Maier, wrote later:

The opening scene showed the home of Dorothy

The cyclone scene from The Wizard of Oz. *A spotlight from the balcony projected clouds onto a gauze curtain.*

Gale...In this serene and peaceful setting the cry "Cyclone" was raised by a dozen farm hands. The stagelights slowly dimmed and in a moment of total darkness, with crashing cimbals [sic] and kettle drums, drowning the terrified voices of the actors, I noted the lowering of a white screen from my perch in the gallery. I cannot say by what magic the illusion of a full-fledged cyclone in action was produced. Still vivid is my recollection of many flying objects, barns, houses, cattle, poultry, and people.

Frank said later, "When the Scarecrow came to life on the first night of *The Wizard of Oz* I expected strange sensations of wonder and awe; the appearance of the Tin Woodman made me catch my breath spasmodically."

Pretty girls in tights, here from The Wizard of Oz, *helped guarantee a show's success.*

Fred Stone's tumble down the rungs of a ladder as the Scarecrow was a highlight of the show. In another scene, the Scarecrow came apart and was put back together by Dorothy and the Tin Woodman.

To attract an adult audience, Mitchell included chorus girls in tights—"more pretty girls than any other show in town," according to one advertisement.

The audience applauded until well after midnight. Frank Jr. told how the crowd clamored, "Author—author!" Then,

> Father slipped from the box, around to the stage entrance . . . and appeared on the stage. He made a delightfully whimsical little speech of thanks for the reception given the play but modestly placed all

From left, *Sir Dashemoff Daily, Dorothy, the Lion, Pastoria, Tryxie Tryfle, and Imogene, all surrounded by Poppy Girls.*

credit for the success upon Julian Mitchell the stage director and the producer, Fred Hamlin.... The house emptied very slowly as though the people hated to leave the atmosphere where they had been so enchanted.

The Chicago *Daily News* called the show spectacular, and continued, "Money fairly drips from the gorgeous walls and skies of the Emerald City and the land of the Munchkins and from the costly robes of the pretty girls and amazing atmospheres of silver mists and golden lights."

Soon there was standing room only at every performance, even in the hottest weather.

Road companies took the show on tour around the country, and it opened in 1903 in New York City. There reviewers judged it out-of-date, but New Yorkers flocked to see it. It had a 293-night run, making it the biggest hit of the decade. Touring companies kept *The Wizard of Oz* alive for nine years.

In The Marvelous Land of Oz, *a boy named Tip makes a pumpkin-headed man and brings him to life with a magic powder.*

SEVEN

Back to Oz

1903-1904

Thanks to the extravaganza *The Wizard of Oz*, Montgomery and Stone became stars. Denslow used profits from the show to buy an island in Bermuda. He called it Denslow Island (it is still known by that name) and proclaimed himself King Denslow the First.

Frank delighted in providing luxuries for his family—a Victrola record player, six bicycles, a motorboat, a player piano, and a Ford automobile.

By this time Frank was a celebrity. Newspapers sent reporters to interview him, and fan letters came from children all over the world. Many urged Frank to write another Oz book.

Frank did not like sequels because he feared getting stuck in a rut. He published a variety of children's books after *The Wonderful Wizard of Oz*, including *A New Wonderland*, the story of a magic kingdom where rain is lemonade

69

and snow is popcorn. This book was later retitled *The Surprising Adventures of the Magical Monarch of Mo.*

The Army Alphabet and *The Navy Alphabet*, both picture books, failed to impress critics. *American Fairy Tales* were too down-to-earth for fantasy fans.

The Master Key: An Electrical Fairy Tale fared better. Frank dedicated this science fiction novel for teenagers to his son Rob.

In the book, the hero, also named Rob, accidentally summons the Demon of Electricity. The Demon gives Rob an electric wristwatch that lets him fly through the air. He gives Rob another machine like a television and video cassette recorder, which shows and records events happening all over the world.

The readers of *St. Nicholas*, a children's magazine, voted *The Master Key* one of their favorite books, but sales fell short of Frank's hopes.

Then Frank's publisher went bankrupt; a new company, Bowen-Merrill, bought the rights to publish and sell *Father Goose* and *The Wonderful Wizard of Oz.* In 1902 this company, later known as Bobbs-Merrill, published Frank's *The Life and Adventures of Santa Claus.*

Two men from the Hill Company soon began a new publishing firm, Reilly & Britton. Both Sumner Charles Britton and Frank Kennicott Reilly had worked for Hill. They were Frank's personal friends, even visiting the Baums at Macatawa.

Now Reilly and Britton took up the cry for a second Oz book—the first title to be published by their new company. They won Maud's support by promising an enthusiastic sales campaign. Frank and Maud had not been satisfied with publicity from either Hill or Bowen-Merrill.

Finally Frank gave in—to a point. He would write a sequel, but he would not bring Dorothy back to Oz—her character was complete in the first book.

The hero of *The Marvelous Land of Oz* is Tip, a boy from the purple Gilliken Country. Tip's guardian is a witch named Mombi. He escapes from her at the story's beginning, and sets off on foot to visit the King, the Scarecrow.

Tip travels with a pumpkin-headed man with a body of wood, made by Tip himself and brought to life with Mombi's magic powder. Later Tip uses the same powder to bring a wooden Saw-Horse to life, and the horse (who can talk, of course) joins the party.

They find the Emerald City under attack by an army of girls, led by General Jinjur. Armed with sharp knitting needles, Jinjur's soldiers conquer the Emerald City, stealing the emeralds for themselves. They liberate the women and force men to take over cooking, cleaning, and child care.

The Scarecrow, Tip, Jack Pumpkinhead, and the Saw-Horse seek help from the Tin Woodman. Next, the group encounters an insect as large as a person. He is H. M. Woggle-Bug, T. E. The initials stand for *H*ighly *M*agnified and *T*horoughly *E*ducated. The Woggle-Bug began life as an ordinary insect, he explains, living in a country schoolhouse. There he acquired an education. One day the professor caught him and projected his image onto a screen through a magnifying glass.

His appearance frightened several students, causing two little girls to fall out a window. Everyone rushed to see if the girls were injured. Left alone and still highly magnified, the Woggle-Bug stepped off the screen and began to travel the world.

The Woggle-Bug joins Tip's party. Soon they are trapped

in the Scarecrow's palace, surrounded by Jinjur and her troops. Now Jinjur has a new ally: Tip's former guardian, the witch Mombi. Tip and his friends build a flying machine to help them escape.

The body of the machine is made of two high-backed sofas bound together with clothesline. Palm leaves make its wings, and a broom becomes its tail. The head is the stuffed head of a Gump (an Oz animal that looks like an elk). After Tip brings the creature to life, the Gump flies our heroes to the palace of Glinda, the great Sorceress.

From reading her history books, Glinda has learned the rightful ruler of Oz is a fairy named Ozma. Ozma, while still a child, was hidden by the Wizard of Oz. No one knows where she is.

Glinda also learns that Mombi had dealings with the Wizard. She captures Mombi and forces her to tell the truth: Mombi hid the girl Ozma by changing her into a boy — Tip!

Reluctantly Tip agrees to be changed back to his natural form. Ozma becomes ruler of Oz with Glinda as her powerful ally. At the end of the book, Oz is indeed taken over by females, but not by Jinjur, who is sent home to her mother.

Frank and Maud took a trip to California in 1904. In a newspaper interview, Frank explained how he thought of the name, the Woggle-Bug:

> "I was out on a California Beach," said L. Frank Baum. "There was a pretty little girl...suddenly she saw one of those little sand crabs, fiddler crabs I suppose they are.
>
> "'Oh, what is it?' she said.
>
> "'A wogglebug,' I said, unthinkingly, using the first term that popped into my head.
>
> "The child was delighted and ran to her parents

The Woggle-Bug and Ozma
were both introduced in the
The Marvelous Land of Oz.

shouting: 'Oh, see what I've got! It's a wogglebug. Mr. Baum says it's a wogglebug.'

"The name was so catchy that the same evening my wife told me I should put the Wogglebug in 'The Marvelous Land of Oz.' The book was one-third written and Jack Pumpkinhead was the hero, but I brought in the Wogglebug right away."

Like Frank, the Woggle-Bug enjoys puns. He warns Jack not to drop his head over the side of the Gump. "In that event," explains the Woggle-Bug, "your head would no longer be a pumpkin, for it would become a squash." Tip eyes him severely, as Frank's sons sometimes regarded their father.

Reilly & Britton hired John R. Neill, a 26-year-old artist from Philadelphia, to illustrate the book. Neill had worked as an artist for several East Coast newspapers. This book was his big break.

Frank did not know Neill; they communicated through their publisher. Neill respected traditions established in the first book, but added his own charming style to Oz.

Once again book reviewers praised both artist and author. They admired the high quality of the book and the unusual color effects, made possible by recent developments in color printing technology.

Tip's change from a boy to a girl follows the dramatic tradition of the "trouser role." A book review in the Cleveland *Leader* objected to the book's theatrical style, saying, "Part of the book, and that the least enjoyable, has been written with a view to the stage. General Jinjur and her soldiers are only shapely chorus girls. The observant reader

Artist John R. Neill (left) *illustrated 13 of Frank's 14 Oz books. For Oz fans, Neill, not Denslow, established the look of Oz and of the strange beings who lived there.* Right: *Frank at age 49.*

This advertisement from Publishers Weekly *announces the success of the new Oz book.*

can see their tights and their ogling glances even in the pages of the book."

Reilly & Britton promoted the new Oz book by publishing an Oz newspaper for children. The *Ozmapolitan*, available in bookstores, kept readers informed of the latest news in the Emerald City.

Frank's next Oz venture involved real newspapers. For six months he wrote a Sunday comic page. In "Queer Visitors from the Marvelous Land of Oz," the Scarecrow, the Tin

Woodman, the Woggle-Bug, Jack Pumpkinhead, and the Saw-Horse fly in the Gump to the United States. Political cartoonist Walt McDougall provided the illustrations. Each week's adventure ended with the riddle, "What Did the Woggle-Bug Say?" Prizes worth $500 a month were awarded to readers who submitted the best answers.

The question became a popular saying in 1904. Later Paul Tietjens set these same words to music, and Frank wrote the lyrics for what became a hit song.

Frank's success as a writer now allowed him to travel, and to live where he liked. By 1904 Frank and Maud had established a pattern that would last for years: summers at Macatawa, autumn through New Year's Day in Chicago, and the rest of the year in the sunshine, in California, the state that became their new home.

EIGHT

Aunt Jane's Nieces

1904-1905

In 1904 Frank and Maud toured the Southwest by automobile. In those days there were no interstate highways, no maps for motorists, no roadside motels. Between cities, travelers sometimes had to camp out.

The Baums traveled from Albuquerque to the Grand Canyon to California, crossing mountains on dirt roads. Sixty miles (95 km) was a good day's trip. This slow pace allowed them to enjoy the scenery.

They ended their trip near San Diego, California. In the years that followed, Frank wrote many books at the Hotel del Coronado, a stylish beach resort with 400 rooms and cottages. By day, guests enjoyed carriage rides on the sand; after dark, they marveled at the electric lights.

When it was built in 1887, the Coronado had more lights than any structure outside New York City. Thomas A. Edison himself had supervised their installation.

The Hotel del Coronado, near San Diego, California, where Frank wrote several Oz books. He and Maud wintered in a cottage on the hotel grounds.

Some claimed Frank based his design of the Emerald City on the Coronado. The hotel says Frank designed the crown-shaped chandeliers in its enormous restaurant, the Crown Room.

Wherever he went, from Michigan to California, Frank received fan mail. In a newspaper interview, he said:

> Not a day passes but I get a letter from a child. They come sometimes singly, sometimes in batches of 50 or 100. Entire classes, where school teachers have read my stories, have written to me. I answer every one personally. When I was a child I know how, if I had received a real letter from an author whose book I'd read, I would have been the happiest boy alive.

In 1905 a newspaper reported that Frank had purchased

an island off the California coast to turn into a Land of Oz playground. There were plans for a large castle and statues of Oz characters. Some said the park would be built on Pedloe Island, but no such island exists on maps. Frank Jr. said later that Pedloe Island was just a publicity stunt.

Paul Tietjens's wife, the poet Eunice Tietjens, noted Frank's love of a good story in her autobiography, *The World at My Shoulder*. She said, "Constantly exercising his imagination as he did, he had come to the place where he could honestly not tell the difference between what he had done and what he had imagined. Everything he said had to be taken with at least a half-pound of salt."

Frank published many non-Oz books in the early 1900s. His *Animal Fairy Tales* were traditional "talking beast" stories. In *The Enchanted Island of Yew*, a girl changes into a boy for an adventure in a magic land. *Queen Zixi of Ix* tries to steal a magic cloak from the little girl who owns it.

John R. Neill illustrated Frank's *John Dough and the Cherub*. John Dough is a live gingerbread man, and Chick the Cherub is the world's first incubator baby. As a gimmick, readers were invited to vote whether Chick was a girl or a boy—ballots were bound into the book.

In *The Woggle-Bug Book*, the Woggle-Bug visits the United States and falls in love with a plaid dress. He has comic adventures as the dress passes from wearer to wearer.

Frank's play *The Woggle-Bug*, based on *The Marvelous Land of Oz*, opened in June 1905 at the Garrick Theatre in Chicago. Once again there were chorus girls dressed as soldiers (Glinda's army) and a comic team—this time Jack Pumpkinhead and the Woggle-Bug.

Critics liked composer Frederic Chapin's music, and the magnification of the Woggle-Bug (by projecting his image on a screen, as in the book). But reviewers called *The Woggle-Bug* a children's show and adults stayed away. It closed in just a month.

Once again Frank was short of money. Reilly & Britton had begun publishing series books for children. Each series followed the same characters through a variety of adventures and settings. Unfortunately most were poorly written compared to Oz books.

Frank started writing several series under different names. He usually reserved L. Frank Baum for fairy tales, which were published regularly, one each Christmas. For other series he became Suzanne Metcalf, Laura Bancroft, Captain Hugh Fitzgerald, and Schuyler Staunton. He wrote the Boy Fortune Hunters series as Floyd Akers.

Using the name Edith Van Dyne, Frank wrote an extremely successful series for teenage girls. The contract for the first book said:

> Baum shall deliver to The Reilly and Britton Co. on or before March 1, 1906 the manuscript of a book for young girls on the style of the Louisa M. Alcott stories, but not so good, the authorship to be ascribed to "Ida May McFarland," or to "Ethel Lynne" or some other mythological female.

The first book, *Aunt Jane's Nieces*, tells of Jane Merrick, a crabby old woman about to die. She summons her three nieces, whom she has never met, to visit her so she can decide who should inherit her money.

All three nieces are poor. Beth is a small-town girl, beautiful but temperamental. She tries to win her aunt's favor by befriending the old woman's elderly servants.

Louise is a glamorous society girl with a secret. She and

Left: *Reilly & Britton printed advertisements in their books for the other books by Frank. This ad appeared in* Aunt Jane's Nieces and Uncle John. Right: *Louise* (left), *Beth, and Patsy with their aunt Jane.*

her widowed mother have decided to spend their meager savings by living luxuriously for three years, until Louise lands a rich husband. Louise tries to charm Aunt Jane into giving her the money.

Patsy, plain and freckled, has red hair and a quick temper. She vows never to accept Aunt Jane's money, remembering that Aunt Jane once refused to help her family.

Aunt Jane receives an unexpected visitor, her long-lost brother, John Merrick. He had left years ago to become a tinsmith in California. Aunt Jane offers the shabby old man a home.

When the old woman dies, the girls discover that Aunt Jane really had no money to leave. Uncle John accepts an invitation to live with Patsy and her father. Their apartment is so small, he has to sleep on the sofa.

The book has a surprise ending: Uncle John is rich— worth more than $80,000,000. He controls most of the canning and tin-plate industries of America. Uncle John buys Patsy a grand apartment, and provides for the other two girls as well.

Later Aunt Jane's Nieces stories are based on experiences in Frank's life. In *Aunt Jane's Nieces and Uncle John*, the characters tour the Southwest and stay at the Hotel del Coronado.

The Aunt Jane's Nieces series earned Frank as much money as did the Oz books. Readers and people in the book trade demanded to meet Edith Van Dyne. One publisher was so persistent that Reilly & Britton arranged a tea and found a woman to play the part of the author. Frank and Maud also attended the party.

Frank and Maud were happy in their middle-aged years. Their sons were young men, each one more than six feet (1.8 meters) tall. Maud was robust, and Frank at this time enjoyed relatively good health. In 1906, with the income from the new series books, they had enough money for a dream trip to a land so exotic it seemed a fantasy world.

NINE

Other Lands

1906

Frank and Maud sailed from New York on the *Princess Irene*, January 28, 1906. Maud wrote from the ship:

> "Life on the ocean wave" is a very lazy existence. A bugle blows at eight to waken us. It gives us half an hour to prepare for breakfast, but generally we don't get up until the second bugle, which announces breakfast at nine. After eating we go on deck to walk, read, or doze, as the mood strikes us. At ten o'clock there is a band concert; at eleven we are served bouillon, crackers, cheese and tongue sandwiches; at one o'clock luncheon is ready, and strange as it may seem we are ready for it. Again we lounge around, reading, writing or chatting with fellow passengers, until afternoon tea overtakes us at four thirty. Then we dress leisurely for a ten or twelve course dinner at seven o'clock, which we devour eagerly because we feel we are nearly famished.

> Afterward they serve us coffee in the smoking-room,
> a pleasant place where many of the ladies go with
> their husbands or escorts to play cards until bed-time.

Although the crossing was rough, neither Frank nor Maud felt seasick. Frank wrote books, even while traveling, and Maud wrote long letters to their sons and other relatives. Later Frank published a book of her letters, entitled *In Other Lands Than Ours*, illustrated by a few of his photographs.

On February 6 the ship stopped at the famous Rock of Gibraltar, between Spain and Morocco at the entrance to the Mediterranean Sea. Europe and Africa are just 23 miles (37 km) apart at this point.

"We are glad we arrived there at night," wrote Maud, "for it was a pretty sight to watch the two or three light-houses on either side of us—Spain on the left and Africa with its mountains on the right. A full moon was over us, and the effect was beautiful."

The next morning Frank and Maud hired a carriage, and toured Gibraltar's narrow streets. They saw "Moors" (North Africans) and also British soldiers, as Gibraltar was an important British fortress.

On February 8 Frank and Maud reached the port city of Alexandria, Egypt. Maud wrote, "The first thing I saw in the famous city of Alexander, Antony and Cleopatra was a Standard Oil tank. My next vision was a line of automobiles on the quay, and these things were as disappointing as they were unexpected."

In Cairo they stayed at Shepheard's Hotel, "quite modernized," according to Maud. The first night, Maud explained, a 60-piece band "saluted our entrance with selections from the 'Wizard of Oz.'"

Frank and Maud pose among ruins in Egypt. This photograph is from Maud's book, In Other Lands Than Ours.

At Shepheard's Hotel, Frank met a little girl from Algeria. With her family she had crossed the desert by camel, and she had been allowed to bring one doll and one book. The book she chose was *The Wonderful Wizard of Oz*.

Frank and Maud hired a dragoman, or guide, to show them Cairo. They toured mosques and bazaars, modern restaurants and Roman ruins. At the Cairo Museum they saw brightly painted mummy cases. The mummies, Maud reported, "turn to a dark leathern hue when exposed to the air."

At the Khedivial Library, they saw books from the 12th century decorated with paints made from crushed rubies, emeralds, and turquoises. The colors still glowed.

Their dragoman also took them to a wedding. At the bride's home, Maud ate with the men, using her hands, as they did, to take food from huge gold and silver dishes. After the meal, slaves poured water over their hands.

Maud visited the harem, or women's quarters. The 16-year-old bride wore white satin and a veil. She was to be her husband's second wife. Although this was the third day of the wedding ceremony, he had never seen her.

The harem rooms were luxurious, and the women there were elegantly clothed. Dancing girls, jugglers, and snake charmers entertained. The harem ladies were surprised that American women did not smoke.

In the harem, harem guards controlled the women. Maud reported, "One of the bejewelled haremites, for some slight misdemeanor, received a severe blow or cuff on the side of her head that nearly knocked her over. Neither she nor any-one else resented it. I was glad when L. F. [Frank], having had enough of the entertainment, sent for us to go home."

On the outskirts of Cairo, Frank and Maud saw the Sphinx and the pyramids. Maud climbed 516 feet (157 meters) to the top of the Great Pyramid, but Frank's heart condition kept him on the ground.

On February 20 they embarked on a cruise up the Nile. This great river flows from south to north for hundreds of miles, emptying into the Mediterranean Sea. Egypt's farm-land is located in a thin green strip on either side of the river, and most of the country's people live in this same area.

In 1906 Egypt was controlled by the British. Frank and Maud traveled on a "great floating hotel," owned by the British firm of Cook's Tours. The steamship *Rameses* carried 70 passengers, mostly Americans.

In Saqqara the steamer stopped so passengers could view two colossal statues. One, of Ramses the Great, was 25 feet (7.6 m) long and in a reclining position. "In order to see the face...," reported Maud, "we climbed upon the huge body and literally 'walked over him.'"

On February 22, the travelers celebrated George Washington's birthday. Maud said, "At dinner L. F. made a neat speech in which he asked all Americans present in this land of tombs to rise and drink a toast to that simple tomb at Mount Vernon so sacred to us all. Every American was on his feet in a second, and the speech made quite a hit."

At some stops the steamship company had donkeys waiting. Frank and Maud rode for miles through barren red rocks in the Valley of the Kings to see tombs of the pharaohs, or Egyptian rulers.

Aswan, 534 miles (860 km) south of Cairo, was the ship's final stop. Four years before the Baums' arrival, a great dam had been built at Aswan to protect the farmland downstream from flooding. Behind the dam, under the lake that had formed, was a flooded city, Philae.

"Only the upper parts of the temples and the kiosk are to be seen," reported Maud. Frank took a snapshot of his wife standing on the roof of a temple, surrounded by water.

The trip upriver took two weeks; the return took six days. Next Frank and Maud sailed for Sicily. They stayed several weeks while Frank finished a book. Then they toured the island with its snow-covered mountains, beautiful cities, and ruins from many ancient cultures.

Nothing could compare to the natural wonder they found in Naples, Italy. They arrived in that city, on the west coast of the Italian mainland, on April 15, just as Mt. Vesuvius erupted. Maud wrote:

> As we landed the sun was shining brilliantly upon a city covered in ashes. Over everything the ashes lie four inches deep, and that is a good deal.

Maud (right) *wrote "We walked on lava so hot that it burned my shoes, and it was still glowing and smoking in places." The colonel who was their guide stands third from the right.*

> Great piles of ashes, many feet high, are being swept into the sides of the road, where they will be carted away in time.
>
> We walked in the park today—ankle deep in ashes, and the trees droop under their weight as snow-covered pines do in mid-winter.

At night the volcano roared like cannons firing, and shot flames into the air. Then the skies were lit for miles around, and hot lava flowed down the mountain. Maud wrote, "The shape of the mountain has changed and it has lost nearly a quarter of its height."

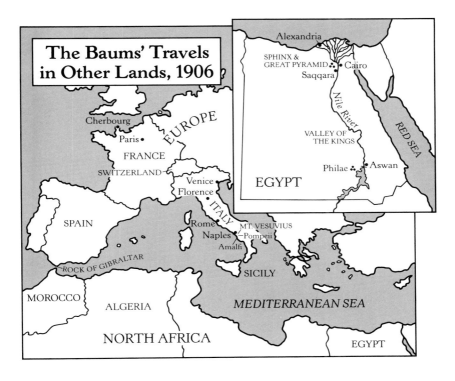

The Baums' Travels in Other Lands, 1906

Frank had a letter of introduction to an Italian colonel, now in charge of relief efforts. The colonel arranged for the Baums to visit places closed to other tourists. In some small villages, banks of dust and ashes were piled so high they reached second-story windows.

Frank and Maud visited Pompeii, an ancient city that had been buried by an explosion of Vesuvius in A.D. 79. From Pompeii they traveled south, along a beautiful ocean road.

"The drive to Amalfi has been our greatest pleasure," wrote Maud. The road, she said, "winds in and out the cliffs and overhangs the sea from one hundred to five hundred feet. The road is on the very edge, being cut from the cliff itself."

In Rome they saw the great outdoor theater known as the Colosseum; the Vatican, the pope's magnificent residence, museums, and offices; and the Forum, the heart of the city in ancient times.

Next, the Baums traveled to Florence. "It combines the modern and the medieval," said Maud, "and this is the time of roses, which bloom everywhere and cover the walls of the lanes and houses with thick masses of flowers." She bought a great bunch of 54 roses for the equivalent of 10 cents.

Maud loved the art in Florence. She was thrilled to see works by Michelangelo, Titian, Raphael, and Leonardo da Vinci, but Frank was less excited. Maud complained: "L. F. grieves me. He says 'he can tell one old master from another as soon as he reads the name on the frame,' and makes other slighting remarks when I grow enthusiastic."

The Baums toured Venice by gondola and by "gasoline launch." They took a train through the Alps to Switzerland. By the time they reached Paris, France, in early June, they were tired of traveling.

Paris disappointed them because it was modern—just like New York or Chicago. They visited traditional tourist sights, the Arc de Triomphe, Napoleon's tomb, the Opera, Notre Dame Cathedral, and the great museum palace, the Louvre.

The Baums sailed home on the steamer *Kaiserin*, departing from the French port of Cherbourg. They had been away five months.

As they neared land, Maud reported, "L. F. said the Statue of Liberty in New York harbor was the most beautiful sight he had seen since he left home."

TEN

Fairylogue and Radio-Plays

1906-1908

In *Aunt Jane's Nieces Abroad*, the second book of the series, a carriage accident on the road to Amalfi leaves the nieces' driver dangling from a cliff until Beth pulls him to safety. In Sicily Uncle John is kidnapped and held for ransom. Patsy befriends the villain's daughter, who masquerades as a boy. Patsy tricks the girl into revealing her father's mountain hideaway; then Patsy and Beth storm the hideout, armed with revolvers.

In Florence Uncle John scoffs at famous paintings: "After all, they're only daubs. Any ten-year-old boy in America can paint better pictures." The sight that pleases him most is the Statue of Liberty.

On November 9, 1907, Frank and Maud celebrated their 25th wedding anniversary. Frank sent out invitations to a party, including this report:

Quarrels: Just a few.
Wife in tears: Three times (cat died; bonnet spoiled,
sore toe).
Husband swore: One thousand one hundred and
eighty-seven times; at wife, 0.
Causes of jealousy: 0. (Remarkable in an age of man-
icured men and beauty
doctor women.)
Broke, occasionally; bent, often.
Unhappy, 0.

With *Ozma of Oz*, the third Oz book, Frank yielded to readers' demands and brought Dorothy back to the series. This story begins with Dorothy and Uncle Henry on an ocean voyage. A storm washes Dorothy overboard, but she saves herself by clinging to a wooden chicken coop, which floats to a beach in Ev, near Oz.

Her companion for this trip is Billina, a yellow hen. Billina and Dorothy realize they are in a fairyland when they discover the hen can talk.

Dorothy and Billina find a mechanical man, Tik-Tok. They meet the Princess Langwidere, who changes heads the way other women change dresses. When Dorothy refuses to swap heads with Langwidere, the Princess locks her in a tower.

Ozma rescues Dorothy when she arrives in Ev with her Army of 27 men—8 Generals, 6 Colonels, 7 Majors, 5 Captains, and 1 private for them all to command. With them are the Scarecrow, the Tin Woodman, and the Cowardly Lion. The Cowardly Lion introduces a new friend, the Hungry Tiger. This tiger longs to eat fat, juicy babies, but his conscience will not let him.

The Oz people have come to save the Queen of Ev and

L. FRANK BAUM'S
New Oz Book
IS
VERY OZZY

The author of THE WIZARD OF OZ and FATHER GOOSE has answered thousands of his little readers' letters by writing

OZMA OF OZ

This new story tells "more about Dorothy," as well as the famous characters of the Scarecrow, the Tin Woodman and the Cowardly Lion and something of several new creations equally delightful, including Tiktok, the machine man, the Yellow Hen, the Nome King and the Hungry Tiger.

The former characters are beloved by multitudes of children and their parents and the new ones, being thoroughly Baumesque, will find their places in the hearts of all.

ILLUSTRATED BY JOHN R. NEILL

Forty-one full-page colored pictures; twenty-two half pages in color and fifty black and white text pictures; special end sheets; title page; copyright page; book plate; dedication page and table of contents.

8vo, 280 pages. Extra cloth binding, side and back stamping in four colors. Uniform in size with The Land of Oz and John Dough and the Cherub.

Price, - - $1.25

Ozma of Oz *introduced a new villain, the Nome King.*

her 10 children, held prisoner by the wicked Nome King in his underground kingdom. (Frank spelled the word *nome* instead of *gnome* because he thought that would be easier for children to read.)

Tik-Tok, Billina, and the Hungry Tiger appear in later Oz books, as does the Nome King, the series's most famous villain. Tik-Tok is known today as one of the first robots in science fiction. Daniel P. Mannix, who has studied Frank's work, claims that although earlier writers invented machine men, Tik-Tok was the first mechanical being who could talk and think.

John R. Neill illustrated *Ozma* and the rest of Frank's Oz books. His art contributed a great deal to the success of the series. In *Ozma* Neill got his first chance to draw Dorothy, who looked different from Denslow's version of the heroine in *The Wonderful Wizard of Oz.*

Neill's Dorothy is older (perhaps nine instead of seven), thinner, and more fashionable. Her hair is blond instead of brown, and her long braids are changed to a stylish bob. Neill patterned his Dorothy after his niece Roberta.

Frank also changed Dorothy for this book, sometimes making her use baby talk. It was then considered cute for little girls to lisp and talk like babies.

But Dorothy's bravery and her common-sense approach to life remained steady. Readers accepted her new look, and *Ozma* proved popular. Frank saved 98 good reviews for his scrapbook.

In 1908 Frank's first grandchild, Joslyn Stanton Baum, was born to Frank Jr. and his wife, Helen. The baby liked to

In The Road to Oz, *Neill's blond Dorothy sees a statue of herself as she first appeared in Oz, and Toto laughs to see the way he used to look. Note seahorse and date on pedestal.*

To My First Grandson
Joslyn Stanton Baum

Frank dedicated his 1909 Oz book, The Road to Oz, *to his new grandson.*

sit on Frank's lap, listening to the ticking of his grandfather's pocket watch. Frank nicknamed him Tik-Tok, and he was known as Tik until he started school.

When Frank's friend had a grandson, Frank wrote:

> Guess like every baby wonder
> He'll be red above and under—
> Take to drinkin'—yell like thunder
> So I s'pose.

With the fourth Oz book, written after the 1906 San Francisco earthquake, Frank brings the Wizard back to Oz. *Dorothy and the Wizard in Oz* is the gloomiest of the series. In it Dorothy and her cat, Eureka, travel to California to visit an uncle. Her cousin Zeb meets them at the train station with a horse and buggy.

Then comes an earthquake! The ground opens and all fall into an underground land. In a second quake the Wizard joins them underground. In his pocket are Nine Tiny Piglets, part of his magic act. Of course all the animals can talk in fairyland.

Dorothy and her companions have landed in the country of the Mangaboos, plant people who hold them responsible for the "rain of stones." The friends escape the Mangaboos only to confront invisible bears, baby dragons, and flying wooden gargoyles. Then Eureka the cat stands trial for murder of a piglet.

As usual, the book was a success. And once again Frank decided to try presenting Oz stories on the stage. This time there were no chorus girls—just a wonderful show for children, with Frank as the star.

Frank financed *Fairylogue and Radio-Plays* himself, with money borrowed from a friend, Harrison Rountree. The show was a travelogue through fairyland. Frank provided the "fairylogue," or narration, accompanied by an orchestra.

Child actors played Oz characters who stepped out of a huge book. Silent movies showed scenes from the first three Oz books and from *John Dough and the Cherub*, and slides promoted *Dorothy and the Wizard in Oz*.

The word *Radio* in the title refers to a Frenchman named Michel Radio. Silent movies were filmed in black and white, but Radio invented a way to hand-color motion picture film. Films for *Fairylogue and Radio-Plays* were made in Chicago, then shipped to Paris to be colored.

The finished film excited audiences with its colors and special effects. These included disappearances, bewitchments, scenes melting into other scenes, a pair of boots that laced themselves, the Gump flapping its palm-leaf wings and flying, and Tip changing into Ozma.

The part of Dorothy went to eight-year-old Romola Remus, who had been acting in movies since the age of three. Frank brought a doll and a box of candy for his "little Dorothy." Romola liked him because he talked to her as to an adult. Later she wrote, "When he came on stage, you could feel that magnetic rapport . . . He was dressed all in white . . . very genteel, with a reserved manner, but without being cold.

Frank poses with actors from Fairylogue and Radio-Plays, *in 1908. The author's costume was a white suit.*

He had warmth and graciousness; I think he loved people very much."

As each show ended, Frank invited children to come onstage to shake hands with Dorothy. Then he autographed books in the theater lobby.

Audiences and critics alike enjoyed *Fairylogue and Radio-Plays*. With Frank Jr. as projectionist, the expensive show toured several states. Frank rented theaters and paid to move actors, scenery, the orchestra, a projector, a metal projection booth (to satisfy fire codes), and a heavy screen. The show closed in December 1908 in New York City.

Frank was broke again.

Title page for The Emerald City of Oz, *1910. Frank tried to end the series with this book.*

ELEVEN

Ozcot

1909-1913

In *The Road to Oz* Dorothy and Toto return to Oz, where they meet a tramp, the Shaggy Man, a lost little boy named Button Bright, and Polychrome, the Rainbow's daughter. The book tells of their adventures on the way to the Emerald City.

The Road to Oz was printed on colored paper. Each section was a different color to match the colors of the countries of Oz.

The book, fifth and weakest of the series, sold well. By this time many parents gave their children Oz books every Christmas. Even brisk sales, however, could not pay the bills for *Fairylogue and Radio-Plays*.

The movies for this show had been made by Selig Polyscope Company of Chicago. To repay Selig, Frank now gave the company these films. Selig released *The Wizard of Oz*, *Dorothy and the Scarecrow in Oz*, *The Land of Oz*, and *John Dough and the Cherub* as four one-reel (short) movies in 1910.

Frank asked Reilly & Britton for advance payment on his next Oz book and they agreed to a monthly salary. Frank, however, still could not pay his debts; in June 1911 he filed for bankruptcy. He listed his assets as two suits of clothes and a typewriter. The story was reported in newspapers across the country.

Frank wrote to a friend, "I am proud to say that I can still claim most of my creditors as personal friends—considerate, patient and sympathetic—and these will readily realize that no action of law can relieve any man from the moral obligation to pay in full his just debts as soon as he is able to do so."

It took years for Frank to repay his friends. The bankruptcy settlement said creditors would be paid with money to be earned from Frank's Bobbs-Merrill books. This meant that Frank received no further royalties from *The Wonderful Wizard of Oz* during his lifetime.

Frank wrote steadily, despite his troubles. In *Aunt Jane's Nieces in Society*, Louise is kidnapped, rescued, and then married. The sixth Oz book was *The Emerald City of Oz*—finally Frank used the name, despite the jewel in the title.

In this book the Nome King tunnels under the Deadly Desert toward the Emerald City. There he plans to retrieve his magic belt, stolen by Dorothy in *Ozma of Oz*. He intends to use the belt to conquer Oz.

Meanwhile Dorothy moves Aunt Em and Uncle Henry to the Emerald City. In a wagon pulled by the Saw-Horse, they tour the Land of Oz with the Shaggy Man and the Wizard.

Dorothy and her party return to the Emerald City just as the Nome King completes his tunnel and appears in the castle garden. Ozma is waiting, having watched his progress in her magic picture. This picture shows her anything she wants to see, anywhere in the world.

With *The Emerald City of Oz*, Frank tried to end the series. At the book's conclusion, the Oz people worry that the coming of airships will cause their fairyland to be overrun by visitors. Glinda casts a spell to render the fairyland invisible, and Dorothy writes to Frank, "You will never hear anything more about Oz, because we are now cut off forever from all the rest of the world. But Toto and I will always love you and all the other children who love us."

The critics did not believe it. "The only graceful way Baum can quit telling tales of Oz is to die," said one. Reilly & Britton hinted that Frank might change his mind later.

By the time this book was published, Frank and Maud had tired of moving from place to place throughout the year. They decided to settle permanently in California, where the warm weather was good for Frank's health.

Frank Jr. and Harry were on their own, but Robert and Kenneth moved with their parents. Frank and Maud hoped that someday all four sons would live near them, so they settled near Los Angeles, where jobs were readily available.

They chose Hollywood, a small suburb surrounded by citrus groves and mountains. The air smelled like orange blossoms and scenic trails led up the hills. Downtown Hollywood was a six-block area, and Vine Street, one of the main thoroughfares, was paved with cobblestones.

Using money Maud had inherited from her mother, the Baums bought a large double lot at 1749 Cherokee Avenue. There they built a two-story frame house, which Frank named Ozcot.

Upstairs were four bedrooms, one being a study for Frank, and a long, enclosed porch overlooking the mountains. Downstairs were a living room, kitchen, library, and a sunroom where Frank grew flowers. One wall was covered with Frank's favorite pictures of his wife. He called this wall his "yard of Maud."

Frank made copper lampshades for the dining room, one for each corner and a large one for the chandelier. He carved the designs himself and installed green glass, so light that showed through would be emerald-colored.

In the yard Frank built an aviary — an enormous circular birdcage. One account says Frank had hundreds of rare, exotic songbirds. He tamed some to sit on his hand or shoulder and to take food from his mouth.

Frank's garden was his greatest pride. Inside a six-foot (1.8-m) redwood fence, paths divided the grounds into sections. A summerhouse stood at the center, surrounded by pools of goldfish and water lilies. An archery range and a separate chicken yard were included. Frank kept Rhode Island Reds for eggs and meat.

Ozcot, the Baums' Hollywood home

Frank in his garden at Ozcot, about 1914. He wore knickers for gardening and to play golf in the afternoons.

He did most of the gardening himself, with a man to cut the grass or help with heavy jobs. Frank planted chrysanthemums in contrasting colors to spell out the word *Oz*. He developed a secret formula for fertilizer. Soon his chrysanthemums and dahlias were winning prizes statewide.

Sometimes children visited Frank in his garden, and he delighted in telling them stories. Occasionally he entertained whole classes with their teachers.

The garden became his study. His son Harry said, "He would make himself comfortable in a garden chair, cross his legs, place the clip board on his knee, and with a cigar in his mouth, begin writing whenever the spirit moved him . . .

"When he finished an episode or adventure, he would get up and work in his garden."

Later Frank typed each book himself, making changes as he worked on the final draft.

Frank (holding Toto), *with Maud's sister Julia, and Maud in the rose garden at Ozcot*

In 1911 Frank published a new children's fantasy, *The Sea Fairies*, illustrated by John R. Neill. In this book mermaids transform a little California girl named Trot and her elderly friend, Cap'n Bill, into a mermaid and merman so they can travel beneath the sea. *The Sea Fairies* sold poorly, and sales for Oz books dropped off, too.

However, Aunt Jane's Nieces earned steady profits. In *Aunt Jane's Nieces on Vacation*, the girls start a newspaper. This book reflects Frank's experience as a newspaper editor in Aberdeen, including his duel over the typographical error.

In Frank's 1912 book, *Sky Island*, Trot and Cap'n Bill travel with a flying umbrella to an island in the sky. That same year Frank yielded to his publisher and fans and began work on the seventh Oz book, *The Patchwork Girl of Oz*. He wrote to his publisher, S. C. Britton:

> The odd characters are a sort of inspiration, liable to strike me any time, but the plot and plan of adventures takes me considerable time to develop. When I get at a thing of that sort I live with it day by day, jotting down on odd slips of paper the various ideas that occur and in this way getting my material together. The new Oz book is in this stage. I've got it all—all the hard work has been done—and it's a dandy I think. But... it's a long way from being ready for the printer yet. I must rewrite it, stringing the incidents into consecutive order, elaborating the characters, etc. Then it's typewritten. Then it's revised, retypewritten and sent on to Reilly & Britton.

In the prologue to *The Patchwork Girl*, Frank tells how he reestablished contact with Oz. A child, he explains, wrote to suggest communicating with Oz via wireless telegraph. So, Frank says, he rigged up a tower in his backyard and took lessons in wireless telegraphy. This enabled the Royal Historian, as he now called himself, to continue the story.

The Patchwork Girl tells of a Munchkin boy named Ojo. He goes on a quest with a large cloth doll brought to life by a magician. Scraps, as she is named, is a boisterous character made from a crazy quilt.

Ojo's uncle and the magician's wife have been turned to stone in an accident. Ojo and Scraps must collect ingredients to bring them back to life. The recipe calls for three hairs from a Woozy's tail. Eventually they find a Woozy, and being unable to pluck the hairs, invite the beast to join them.

Reviewers liked *The Patchwork Girl*. When it was finished, Frank turned again to the theater. Drama was changing, thanks to a new technology, and Frank would soon be caught up in the change.

Officers of the Oz Film Manufacturing Company. From left: *Clarence Rundel, L. Frank Baum, H. M. Walderman, Louis F. Gottschalk.*

TWELVE

The Oz Film Manufacturing Company

1913-1915

On March 31, 1913, a new musical, *The Tik-Tok Man of Oz*, opened at Morosco's Majestic Theatre in Los Angeles. Oliver Morosco was a well-known producer and theater owner, Frank's new friend from the Los Angeles Athletic Club.

In this play a little girl named Betsy Bobbin travels to Oz by way of shipwreck, accompanied by her pet mule, Hank. They meet the Shaggy Man, who wants to rescue his brother from the Nome King. They also meet Polychrome, Tik-Tok, and Queen Ann of Oogaboo. Queen Ann hires Tik-Tok as the only private in her army. All the other soldiers are officers. Ann hopes to conquer the Nome King by invading his underground kingdom.

The show's special effects were outstanding. In one scene travelers crossed a chasm on the stage, using a rainbow for a bridge. The rainbow was projected onto the stage by passing a light through a prism. Actually actors crossed the chasm on a board bridge, which could not be seen in the bright light.

In the Nome King's cavern, huge "jewels" were lit from within by electric lights. The nomes were played by—what else?—pretty girls in tights.

Audiences flocked to see the show in San Francisco and Chicago, but Chicago critics complained that the extravaganza style was out of date. Producer Morosco closed the show in the summer, while it was still earning a profit. Frank reused the plot for his eighth Oz book, *Tik-Tok of Oz*.

By 1914 Hollywood had changed dramatically from the quiet town where Frank and Maud had settled in 1910. Frank described later what happened:

> A score or more of motion picture makers . . . were utilizing the brilliant sunshine and clear atmosphere in the production of their films . . . Appreciating the value of such a monster industry, the authorities permitted the cameras to be set upon the public streets or wherever there was an appropriate scene to serve for a background to the photo-plays. It was no unusual sight to see troops of cowboys and Indians racing throughout the pretty village or to find the cameraman busy before the imposing residence of a millionaire or the vine-covered bungalow of a more modest citizen.

Land was cheap in Hollywood. Filmmakers bought huge lots and constructed enormous buildings. Frank met many men connected with the movie industry at the Los Angeles Athletic Club, among them, cowboy star Will Rogers and actor George Arliss.

Soon Frank and his friends formed a smaller group within the Athletic Club, known as the Uplifters. Frank made

Frank (on the table) *poses for a publicity photo advertising a show by the Uplifters. He played a gambler.*

up titles for the Uplifters' officers: Grand Muscle (president), Elevator (vice president), Royal Hoister (secretary), Lord High Raiser (treasurer), and the Excelsiors (board of directors).

Sometimes the Uplifters presented plays for the rest of the Athletic Club. Frank wrote scripts and song lyrics. In "Somewhere by the Sea," he played a gambler, and his songs were performed by the Whooping Cough Quartette.

Soon the Uplifters began making movies together, based on Oz books. Frank became president of the new Oz Film Manufacturing Company. Louis F. Gottschalk, an Uplifter who had written the music for *The Tik-Tok Man of Oz*, was vice president, and Frank Jr. served for a time as general manager.

Instead of investing his own money in this company, Frank Sr. received stock in the company (and thus a share in the profits) in exchange for the movie rights to his books.

The company bought a seven-acre (2.8-hectare) lot opposite the Universal Film Company in Hollywood. A high board fence surrounded the Oz lot; a tunnel under the lot allowed for special effects. Thanks to the tunnel, armies could appear and disappear with ease, and rivers could be made to flow through a series of tanks.

Frank and his friends began filming *The Patchwork Girl of Oz*. It took about a month to make this five-reel, feature-length film. The cast included Fred Woodward, King of Animal Interpreters, as Hank the Mule and the Woozy. The Patchwork Girl was played by a 17-year-old French acrobat, Pierre Couderc.

Frank needed a distributor to send his movie to theaters. While he tried to find one, the Oz film company completed a second movie, *The Magic Cloak*, based on *Queen Zixi of Ix*. Then they began work on a third, *His Majesty, the Scarecrow of Oz*. This film had a cast of 130 people and cost $23,500 to make—a huge sum at that time.

In this film, a man-sized crow carries off the Scarecrow, a witch is sealed in a tin can, and a princess's heart is frozen by a magic spell.

Frank reworked the plot of this movie for his 1915 Oz book *The Scarecrow of Oz*. In it Trot and Cap'n Bill travel to

Oz for the first time. Glinda sends the Scarecrow to help them to defeat a cruel king.

Finally Paramount, a distributor, agreed to release *The Patchwork Girl of Oz*. Audiences decided the film was strictly for children, and some adults even demanded refunds. Paramount refused to release any more Oz films.

Maud, as always, tried to cheer Frank. When she went on a trip, he wrote to her:

> Yes, sweetheart, nothing can dismay us while we have each other and while the old love, which has lasted and grown stronger during all these years, remains to comfort and encourage us . . .
>
> I don't believe I'll ever let you go away from me again. I miss you too much.

Frank and Maud (seated) *surrounded by their family on Thanksgiving Day 1915*

A still from the Oz Film Manufacturing Company's film His Majesty, the Scarecrow of Oz. Left to right: *The Tin Woodman, Gardener Pon, the Scarecrow, and Dorothy.*

The Alliance Film Corporation released *His Majesty, the Scarecrow of Oz* after renaming it *The New Wizard of Oz.* The film was shown under that title as late as 1920.

Frank wrote a film called *The Last Egyptian*, based on his adult novel of the same title. Next the company made *The Gray Nun of Belgium*, a war story. After these films failed, Frank and his friends gave up making movies and sold the Oz studios to Universal.

Even though Frank had not lost money on the films, Maud was worried. She demanded that future royalty checks be made out to her. Frank did not object. His business failures had affected his health, and his heart was growing weaker.

He suffered also from gallbladder attacks and from a condition known as tic douloureux. This caused painful spasms in his face; they came and went with no warning. He carried on bravely, but sometimes, when he wrote, his paper was wet with tears. Frank wasted no time on self-pity.

There were larger problems than his, he knew—the world was at war. When the Great War, now known as World War I, began in 1914, it seemed far away in Europe. But as years passed, the war made claims on every American family.

Frank in his bed at Ozcot. He hated pajamas and always wore a nightshirt.

THIRTEEN

The Great War

1915-1919

A*unt Jane's Nieces in the Red Cross* sends the girls to war. When this book was published in 1915, the United States was still neutral. Uncle John and the girls convert a yacht into a hospital ship. They sail for Europe, where they treat the injured from both sides. After three months, they go home, certain that the war will soon end.

Frank's 1915 Oz book, *The Scarecrow of Oz*, was his favorite. It is dedicated to the Uplifters. Reviewers liked it. The Chicago *Tribune* praised the book's most unusual character, saying, "In *The Scarecrow of Oz*, the 'Ork,' a four-legged 'bird' with a propeller for a tail, has been discovered to add new joy to the thousands of little tots who devour these remarkable narratives."

Because *Tik-Tok of Oz* (1914) had sold poorly, Reilly & Britton began a major sales campaign for *The Scarecrow*. To advertise the series, the firm published a 16-page book, illustrated by John R. Neill, *The Oz Toy Book, Cut-outs for the Kiddies*. But they neglected to inform Frank of this plan, which he discovered by reading a Reilly & Britton catalog. Frank protested angrily the unauthorized use of characters he had created, and Reilly & Britton apologized to their star author.

Frank's health was so poor after he completed *The Scarecrow* that he gave up writing for a time. His heart condition grew worse. Doctors advised him to live quietly, to avoid smoking, and to watch his weight.

But Frank loved to eat three heavy meals each day. He suffered afterward from nausea and stomach pains, symptoms of angina pectoris and an inflamed gallbladder. Physicians wanted to remove his gallbladder, but Frank refused. Instead, he treated himself with patent medicines and somehow grew better.

He resumed writing with *Rinkitink in Oz*. He had written much of this story years before, as a non-Oz book. *Rinkitink* tells the story of Prince Inga, who must save his kingdom with the help of a neighboring king, Rinkitink. To this story, Frank added Dorothy and the Emerald City at the end. Although children never tired of Oz books, a critic from the Buffalo *Express* wrote, "Oh, well, just to tell it is enough, so listen: There's another Oz book out. It's the real thing, for L. Frank Baum wrote it. The title? Oh, yes. That is a matter of some interest. Well, it's *Rinkitink in Oz*. And now we are off."

Frank's gallbladder attacks grew worse. He was in constant pain while he worked on *The Lost Princess of Oz*, published in 1917. In this mystery someone steals Ozma's magic picture, Glinda's Great Book of Records, the Wizard's magic tools, and even Ozma herself. Dorothy, wearing the

Glinda reads her Great Book of Records, which records every event that takes place anywhere, just as it happens.

Nome King's magic belt, leads a search party to find her friend.

In 1918 Frank agreed to have his gallbladder removed. By this time he had written two extra Oz books, *The Magic of Oz* and *Glinda of Oz*, and stored them in a safe-deposit box as a kind of insurance. They were to be published if he became too ill to write a new book each year.

Frank stayed in the hospital for several weeks after his surgery, then returned to Ozcot, accompanied by a nurse. Because his heart had weakened, he became an invalid.

He did not complain, but tried to adjust to his new way of life by writing a little each day. Propped up on pillows, he finished *The Tin Woodman of Oz* for a 1918 publication date.

In this book the Tin Woodman visits his old home, where he changed from a human being to a man of tin. Before he met Dorothy in the first book, his ax had chopped off parts of his body. A tinsmith replaced the parts, but in Oz, the parts did not die. In an extraordinary scene, the Tin Woodman chats with his former head, now kept in a cupboard.

The United States had entered the war in 1917. In a review of *The Tin Woodman, Publishers Weekly* magazine said, "There is one country where no shadow has been cast by the war; it is the Land of Oz."

Frank and Maud had two sons in the service. Rob was an officer in the Engineer Corps and Frank Jr. was an officer of heavy artillery in France. Frank wrote to him in September 1918:

> We were sorry to learn of your great disappointment in certain phases of your military assignment. But do not be too down-hearted, my boy, for I have lived long enough to learn that in life nothing adverse lasts very long. And it is true, that as the years pass, and we look back on something which, at the time, seemed unbelievedly [sic] discouraging and unfair, we come to realize that, after all, God was at all times on our side . . . .
>
> I have lately improved much in health and trust that before many weeks the doctors will allow me to leave my bed and at least move about the house.
>
> We all send you much love and I continually pray for a speedy end to this terrible war and your safe return to our beloved country.
>
> Your loving and devoted,
>
> > Dad.

In 1918 Reilly & Britton published an updated version of *Aunt Jane's Nieces in the Red Cross*. In his introduction, which was the same in both editions, Frank (as Edith Van Dyne) wrote:

Aunt Jane's Nieces in the Red Cross *was by far the most serious book in the series.*

This is the story of how three brave American girls sacrificed the comforts and luxuries of home to go abroad and nurse the wounded soldiers of a foreign war.

I wish I might have depicted more gently the scenes in hospital and on battlefield, but it is well that my girl readers should realize something of the horrors of war, that they may unite with heart and soul in earnest appeal for universal, lasting Peace and the future abolition of all deadly strife.

However, in the first edition of this book, war was a noble idea. Hospital and battlefield scenes were mild compared to those in the second version. In the first, the men who die are unknown soldiers. In the 1918 edition, Red Cross workers find an old acquaintance, an American cameraman, terribly wounded. "When they came to his right side the flesh was riddled and his right arm a pulp of mangled flesh and bone." Later they must tell him that his arm has been amputated.

The second edition ends the series, with Patsy and Beth grown up, doing important work. Both are engaged to be married after the war is over. Instead of going home after three months, as they did in the first edition, the young women decide to stay in Europe for as long as they are needed.

Frank revised *The Magic of Oz* throughout 1918. This was one of the books from his safe-deposit box. He could not forget the war, even in this fairy tale. The book is dedicated to the children of "our Soldiers, the Americans and their Allies."

In this story the Nome King tries again to conquer Oz, with a magic word, "Pyrzqxgl," that lets him make transformations. Frank warns his readers:

> Now, of course, I would not dare to write down this magic word so plainly if I thought my readers would pronounce it properly and so be able to transform themselves, but it is a fact that no one in all the world . . . had ever (up to the time this story begins) been able to pronounce "Pyrzqxgl" the right way, so I think it is safe to give it to you. It might be well, however, in reading this story aloud, to be careful not to pronounce Pyrzqxgl the proper way, and thus avoid all danger of the secret being able to work mischief.

The Magic of Oz has a double plot. While the Nome King prepares for battle, Trot and Cap'n Bill seek a birthday present for Ozma. On a tiny island they find a Magic Flower that constantly changes its blossoms.

In the real world, the Great War was finally ending. In

the fall of 1918, the Central Powers (Germany and its allies) surrendered. The official treaty was signed the following year.

Frank's health grew steadily worse and he seldom left his bed. The nurse who had accompanied him home from the hospital stayed on and on. She cared for him as his heart grew weaker and he suffered the pains of tic douloureux. It grieved him that he could no longer answer letters from children. Sometimes he was so ill that he did not know people for weeks at a time.

Occasionally he felt better. He worked then, revising *Glinda of Oz*, the other book written before his surgery. He courted Maud, as he always had. She wrote later, "I am very fond of candy and he always gave me a two lb. box of the very best up to the week he passed on."

For the last 18 months of his life, Frank sustained himself by his sheer will to live. On May 5, 1919, he suffered a stroke. Maud and the nurse realized he was dying. Though he could barely speak, Frank reassured Maud that she could keep the house, and that royalties from his books would support her for years to come. Then he lapsed into unconsciousness.

Frank died quietly the next day, May 6. At the end he mumbled in his coma, then he opened his eyes and said clearly, "Now we can cross the Shifting Sands."

Maud (shown about 1939) preserved Oz for new generations by allowing Frank's publishers to add to the series after his death.

FOURTEEN

Follow the
Yellow Brick Road

1919-

The Uplifters attended Frank's funeral. He was buried in Forest Lawn Memorial Park, at Glendale, California. The simple marker reads:

L. FRANK BAUM
1856-1919

Ten days after Frank's death, Maud wrote to her sister, Helen Leslie Gage:

> He told me many times I was the only one he had ever loved. He hated to die, did not want to leave me, said he was never happy without me, but it was better he should go first, if it had to be, for I doubt if he could have got along without me. It is all so sad, and I am so forlorn and alone. For nearly thirty-seven years we had been everything to each other, we were happy, and now I am alone, to face the world alone.

The Magic of Oz appeared in bookstores soon after Frank's death. The New York *Sun* lamented, "The wonderful land will yield no more of its magical secrets; this is the end of the trail."

But there was still one more Oz book, the second title from Frank's safe-deposit box. *Glinda of Oz* was published in 1920, the same year that women finally won the right to vote in the United States.

Glinda of Oz begins as Dorothy and Ozma travel to the land of the Flatheads and the Skeezers, to make peace between the two warring nations.

This book, dedicated to Frank's son Rob, borrows one of Rob's ideas, an alarm system. The Flatheads live on top of a mountain reached by steps leading through the center. To guard against invaders, an alarm bell rings on the mountain top whenever someone reaches a landing on the stairs.

The Skeezers live on a glass-covered island in the middle of a lake. The island can be raised and lowered by magical machinery. Submerged, the island resembles the underwater city of Philae, which Frank and Maud saw in Egypt.

Reilly & Lee (formerly Reilly & Britton) decided that the Oz series was too profitable to end. Maud still received royalties from Frank's Oz books. When the publishers promised her royalties from future Oz books, too, she agreed to let them find a new Royal Historian.

Twelve-year-old Jack Snow wrote to Reilly & Lee offering his services. Frank Jr. also wanted the job, but the publishers chose an established children's writer, Ruth Plumly Thompson.

Thompson's first Oz book was *The Royal Book of Oz.* Publicity claimed she based the story on notes left by Frank, but Thompson wrote the entire book herself.

Ruth Plumly Thompson with actors from her play A Day in Oz. *They played in department stores to promote Oz books. John R. Neill wrote to his publishers: "Congratulations on having secured an author of such superior qualifications to continue the work of supplying the 'Oz books.'"*

John R. Neill continued to illustrate the series, and Oz books, old and new, sold steadily. Thompson wrote 18 more yearly Oz books (Frank wrote 14 in all) before retiring as Royal Historian in 1939. She published one last Oz book in 1972, and in 1976 an unpublished manuscript was issued by the International Wizard of Oz Club. Although she never met Maud, they corresponded.

Over the years many other writers published Oz books, including John R. Neill, Jack Snow, Rachel Cosgrove, Dick Martin, and Eloise Jarvis McGraw and Lauren McGraw Wagner. In 1989, Frank's great-grandson, Roger Baum, wrote *Dorothy of Oz.* All these later books were generally dismissed by critics as inferior to Thompson's. Some purists insist that L. Frank Baum wrote the only real Oz books.

Above: *Listeners of the radio show could send in Jell-O box fronts for books like this.* Left: *One listener could recall vividly as an adult hearing the Wizard "cutting through the sorcerer Gwig and finding him to be like a potato inside."*

Oz was adapted to many different uses. In 1928 Jean Gros's French Marionettes toured the country with a musical puppet show, *The Magical Land of Oz,* by Ruth Plumly Thompson.

The first Oz radio shows aired in the 1920s, in Chicago and New York. Maud owned radio rights to all Oz books, including those by Thompson. In 1933 Maud received $300 a week for a program broadcast on 25 stations across the United States. Jell-O was the sponsor.

In 1925 Frank Jr. wrote the screenplay for a new movie of *The Wizard of Oz*. Chadwick Pictures produced this film for its star, Larry Semon, who played the Scarecrow. Oliver Hardy, who later became half of the famous comedy team, Laurel and Hardy, played the Tin Woodman. The movie was so bad that children wrote to Ruth Plumly Thompson to protest.

In 1933 Ted Eshbaugh produced a short cartoon version of *The Wizard*, in color, with sound. Because of legal complications it was never released.

By this time Maud had regained the copyright, including movie rights, to *The Wonderful Wizard of Oz*. Many people, including Ruth Plumly Thompson, thought Shirley Temple, Hollywood's biggest star, would be perfect as Dorothy. However, Temple's studio did not offer Maud enough money, and for $40,000 Metro-Goldwyn-Mayer (MGM) bought the rights to make a movie of the book.

Maud's memories of earlier Oz films gave her little hope for the new one. When producer Mervyn LeRoy asked her what she expected, she replied, "Oh, I suppose there'll be a Wizard in it, and a Scarecrow and a Tin Woodman, and maybe a Lion and a character named Dorothy. But that's all I expect, young man. You see, I've lived in Hollywood since 1910."

Many books have been written about the making of this movie (see page 139). Oz fans protested when the movie "explained" Oz as a dream. Some thought 16-year-old Judy Garland was too old to play Dorothy. She had to wear a special corset to flatten her chest.

But her wonderful performance made Garland a star. Ray Bolger as the Scarecrow, Jack Haley as the Tin Man, Bert Lahr as the Cowardly Lion, and Margaret Hamilton as

Photos from the 1939 MGM movie The Wizard of Oz. *Above, left to right:* Ray Bolger *as the Scarecrow,* Judy Garland *as Dorothy,* Bert Lahr *as the Cowardly Lion, and* Jack Haley *as the Tin Woodman.* Below: The Wicked Witch, *Margaret Hamilton, melts.*

the Wicked Witch were identified with those roles for the rest of their lives.

Maud attended the Hollywood premiere of *The Wizard of Oz* at Grauman's Chinese Theatre in Hollywood on August 15, 1939. Also attending was Fred Stone, the Scarecrow from Frank's 1902 extravaganza. Thousands of people jammed streets around the theater and roofs of nearby buildings. Klieg lights shone on the skies overhead, while little people dressed as Munchkins greeted arriving guests.

Audiences loved the film, but some critics did not. "A stinkeroo," said *The New Yorker*. "[It] displays no trace of imagination, good taste, or ingenuity."

The movie was rereleased in 1949 and again in 1955, but yearly showings on television made it a classic. Now more people have seen this movie than have seen any other movie in the world. In 1989 Librarian of Congress James H. Billington declared *The Wizard of Oz* one of 25 film titles to be protected as "national treasures" under the National Film Preservation Act of 1988.

Maud died in 1953, a year before Walt Disney bought movie rights to the remaining Oz books. Disney worked on an Oz television special but never completed it. Other producers made television versions of Oz stories, including a *Land of Oz* show with a grown-up Shirley Temple playing Tip and Ozma.

In 1956 Columbia University Libraries celebrated the centenary (100th anniversary) of Frank's birth with a display of L. Frank Baum materials. A catalog accompanying the exhibit explained:

> After the exhibition was installed and the catalogue copy was in the hands of the printer, we were

The International Wizard of Oz Club publishes The Baum Bugle *three times a year.*

visited by Mr. Justin Schiller, aged 12, who, it developed, is an ardent collector of L. Frank Baum. He brought with him a number of significant items, some of which we had sought for vainly when the exhibition was being prepared, and some which we had not known existed. Mr. Schiller has graciously permitted us to include selected items from his library in this display; the printer, in his turn, has agreed to the insertion of this *Addenda.*

In 1957 Justin Schiller organized the International Wizard of Oz Club, with 16 charter members. Schiller began publishing the club's journal, *The Baum Bugle*, that same year. By 1991, the club had more than 3,000 members.

A feature cartoon, *Journey Back to Oz*, was released to movie theaters in 1972. In 1975 a musical, *The Wiz*, became a hit on Broadway. The 1978 film version of this musical earned poor reviews, though Michael Jackson received praise as the Scarecrow.

In 1985 Walt Disney Pictures released a $25,000,000

feature-length film, *Return to Oz*. Based on *The Marvelous Land of Oz* and *Ozma of Oz*, this film combines live action and animation. Parts of the movie offended those who loved the books. Aunt Em, refusing to believe Dorothy's story about her first trip to Oz, commits her to a mental institution where she will receive terrifying shock treatments. This betrayal of a child by a trusted adult goes against all the rules established in Frank's work. Oz fans and critics gave the movie mixed reviews.

Today Oz books are still selling. *The Wonderful Wizard of Oz* has been translated into many foreign languages. In the Soviet Union the book is used to teach children English. In the Russian language, Munchkins are known as the Chewing People. In the Chinese version of *The Wizard*, the lion resembles a dragon.

The 1990 NBC television movie The Dreamer of Oz *told the story of Frank's life. Frank was played by John Ritter.*

Oz is known around the world. Frank's characters and ideas pop up everywhere, in editorial cartoons, advertisements, and in the games small children invent for themselves. The MGM movie has acquired a cult status of its own. Lines from this film ("I'm melting") are recognized instantly with no explanation needed.

L. Frank Baum's reputation as a writer is based on the literary awareness of children, who always understood better than did adults the value of his work. Frank states in the introduction to *Dorothy and the Wizard in Oz*:

> I believe, my dears, that I am the proudest story-teller that ever lived. Many a time tears of pride and joy have stood in my eyes while I read the tender, loving, appealing letters that come to me in almost every mail from my little readers. To have pleased you, to have interested you, to have won your friendship, and perhaps your love, through my stories, is to my mind as great an achievement as to become President of the United States. Indeed, I would much rather be your story-teller, under these conditions, than to be the President. So you have helped me to fulfill my life's ambition, and I am more grateful to you, my dears, than I can express in words.

L. Frank Baum lives now in the hearts of children, young and old. The Royal Historian of Oz will live forever, like the wonderful characters and the magic land he created.

FIFTEEN

Afterword
Oz and the Censors

Readers may not realize that Oz books have been censored almost from the start of the series.

Even in Frank's lifetime, some libraries refused to buy Oz books. Fantasy was unpopular in the early 1900s. Educators thought children should read realistic books with useful lessons. They did not understand that the Oz books taught important values subtly, through humor.

Series books had bad reputations. Some librarians complained that if a child read one Oz book, that child expected to read them all! The books were so popular with readers that they wore out quickly, and replacing so many books by the same author cost too much.

Oz and the censors made headlines in 1957. Claiming Oz books had "a cowardly approach to life," Detroit Library Director Ralph Ulveling removed them from the library's children's departments.

The Detroit Times responded by publishing *The Wonderful Wizard of Oz* in serial installments, stating this was the book the city's library had banned.

Then Florida State Librarian Dorothy Dodd made news when she listed Oz and other series as "poorly written, untrue to life, sensational, foolishly sentimental and consequently unwholesome for the children in your community." She urged Florida libraries to remove these books from their collections.

Children, who loved Oz, responded by saving their allowances for Oz books, or by asking Santa for them, and then trading the books among themselves.

Oz is still under attack. In the 1980s, some critics called parts of Frank's work offensive. They said characters from *The Patchwork Girl*, the live phonograph and the Tottenhots, were stereotypes of African Americans. However, these same critics called Frank decent and mild compared to other authors of his time.

In 1986, seven fundamentalist Christian families filed suit against public schools in Tennessee. They objected to having *The Wizard of Oz* as required reading in elementary classes.

The parents did not want their children reading about witches. They complained that, in Oz, females assume traditional male roles, and animals are elevated to human status. The judge ruled that these parents could remove their children from class when such materials were used.

Frank had many defenders over the years. At first, scholars ignored Oz as just another series. But in 1927 Edward Wagenknecht, a professor at the University of Seattle, and an Oz fan as a child, called Oz "an important pioneering work." Wagenknecht praised Frank's creation of uniquely American characters such as the Scarecrow, and Frank's American style of magic, based on everyday objects and machinery.

In 1946 *Collier's* magazine wrote of *The Wonderful Wizard of Oz*, "Many children's books each year are ballyhooed by critics as something stupendous, but this particular one, which critics and serious thinkers never did value much, goes on seemingly forever."

In 1959 the Henry Regnery Company purchased Reilly & Lee. They reissued the Oz books and published a 1961 biography of Frank, *To Please a Child*, by Russell P. MacFall and Frank Jr.

This biography, with other scholarly articles from the 1950s and 1960s, recognized Frank as a major American author. Science fiction authors, especially, acknowledged his influence on their style of writing.

Libraries established Baum collections in Aberdeen, South Dakota; Evansville, Indiana; Milwaukee, Wisconsin; and at Columbia, Yale, and Syracuse Universities.

In 1973 Frank won new respect in the book *The Annotated Wizard of Oz*. Author Michael Patrick Hearn added information about Frank's life and writings to the story.

Frank's reputation grew during the 1970s, especially because of the women's movement. Dorothy was a good role model for girls, said feminists, and for boys, too.

In the 1980s, many fans knew Oz books only from small paperback editions with black-and-white illustrations. John R. Neill's beautiful color pictures were simply omitted. Then Books of Wonder began publishing full-size Oz books with color plates, giving young readers and librarians their first chance to see the books as Neill designed them.

Children have always loved Oz, and their love kept the Oz books in print. Frank's first readers grew up to become authors, teachers, judges, scientists, librarians, and parents

The Oz books are available in different editions, with different illustrations, in most libraries in the United States.

who read to their children. Now Frank is known as an influential American writer. The Oz books are considered classics, books that changed children's literature forever.

Most libraries own at least one version of *The Wizard of Oz,* and many are buying the sequels. Respect for L. Frank Baum and the new availability of Oz mean that some day library patrons everywhere may be able to check out Frank's whole series—14 of the best-loved, best-selling books ever published for children.

Major Sources for This Book

Aberdeen Saturday Pioneer. Aberdeen, South Dakota. Various dates.

American Book Collector. December 1962. Special L. Frank Baum issue.

Baum, Frank Joslyn, and Russell P. MacFall. *To Please a Child: A Biography of L. Frank Baum Royal Historian of Oz*. Chicago: Reilly & Lee, 1961.

Baum, Harry Neal. Articles in *The Baum Bugle* and the *American Book Collector*.

Baum, Maud Gage. *In Other Lands Than Ours* (1907). Delmar, New York: Scholars' Facsimiles & Reprints, 1983.

Baum, Robert Stanton. Articles in *The Baum Bugle*.

The Baum Bugle and *The Best of the Baum Bugle*. Kinderhook, Illinois: The International Wizard of Oz Club, 1957 to date.

Eyles, Allen. *The World of Oz*. Tucson: HPBooks, 1985.

Gardner, Martin, and Russell B. Nye. *The Wizard of Oz and Who He Was*. East Lansing, Michigan: Michigan State University Press, 1957.

Greene, David L., and Dick Martin. *The Oz Scrapbook*. New York: Random House, 1977.

Hearn, Michael Patrick. Introduction, notes, and bibliography for *The Annotated Wizard of Oz*. New York: Clarkson Potter, 1973.

L. Frank Baum Collection. Alexander Mitchell Library, Aberdeen, South Dakota.

L. Frank Baum Papers. George Arents Research Library for Special Collections at Syracuse University, Syracuse, New York.

Mannix, Daniel P. "The Father of the Wizard of Oz." *American Heritage*, December 1964, 36-47, 108-109.

Matilda Jewell Gage Collection. The Arthur and Elizabeth Schlesinger Library, Radcliffe College, Cambridge, Massachusetts.

Moore, Raylyn. *Wonderful Wizard, Marvelous Land*. Bowling Green, Ohio: Bowling Green University Popular Press, 1974.

Onondaga Historical Association, Syracuse, New York.

Wagenknecht, Edward. *Utopia Americana*. Seattle: University of Washington Bookstore, 1929.

And, of course, the works of L. Frank Baum.

The Books of L. Frank Baum
A Selected List

The Oz Series:
The Wonderful Wizard of Oz, 1900. Illustrated by W. W. Denslow
The Marvelous Land of Oz, 1904. Illustrated by John R. Neill
Ozma of Oz, 1907. Illustrated by John R. Neill
Dorothy and the Wizard in Oz, 1908. Illustrated by John R. Neill
The Road to Oz, 1909. Illustrated by John R. Neill
The Emerald City of Oz, 1910. Illustrated by John R. Neill
The Patchwork Girl of Oz, 1913. Illustrated by John R. Neill
Tik-Tok of Oz, 1914. Illustrated by John R. Neill
The Scarecrow of Oz, 1915. Illustrated by John R. Neill
Rinkitink in Oz, 1916. Illustrated by John R. Neill
The Lost Princess of Oz, 1917. Illustrated by John R. Neill
The Tin Woodman of Oz, 1918. Illustrated by John R. Neill
The Magic of Oz, 1919. Illustrated by John R. Neill
Glinda of Oz, 1920. Illustrated by John R. Neill

The Aunt Jane's Nieces Series (as Edith Van Dyne):
Aunt Jane's Nieces, 1906
Aunt Jane's Nieces Abroad, 1906
Aunt Jane's Nieces at Millville, 1908
Aunt Jane's Nieces at Work, 1909
Aunt Jane's Nieces in Society, 1910
Aunt Jane's Nieces and Uncle John, 1911
Aunt Jane's Nieces on Vacation, 1912
Aunt Jane's Nieces on the Ranch, 1913
Aunt Jane's Nieces Out West, 1914
Aunt Jane's Nieces in the Red Cross, 1915, 1918

Other Books:
American Fairy Tales, 1901. Illustrated by Harry Kennedy, Ike Morgan, N.P. Hall
The Army Alphabet, 1900. Illustrated by Harry Kennedy

The Art of Decorating Dry Goods Windows and Interiors, 1900

The Book of the Hamburgs, 1886

By the Candelabra's Glare, 1898. Illustrated by W.W. Denslow and others

Dot and Tot of Merryland, 1901. Illustrated by W. W. Denslow

The Enchanted Island of Yew, 1903. Illustrated by Fanny Y. Cory

Father Goose, His Book, 1899. Illustrated by W. W. Denslow

John Dough and the Cherub, 1906. Illustrated by John R. Neill

A Kidnapped Santa Claus, 1904, 1969. Illustrated by Richard Rosenblum

The Life and Adventures of Santa Claus, 1902. Illustrated by Mary
    Cowles Clark

The Master Key: An Electrical Fairy Tale, 1901. Illustrated by
    Fanny Y. Cory

Mother Goose in Prose, 1897. Illustrated by Maxfield Parrish

The Navy Alphabet, 1900. Illustrated by Harry Kennedy

Queen Zixi of Ix, 1905. Illustrated by Frederick Richardson

The Sea Fairies, 1911. Illustrated by John R. Neill

Sky Island, 1912. Illustrated by John R. Neill

The Surprising Adventures of the Magical Monarch of Mo and His People,
    1903. Illustrated by Frank Verbeck

About the MGM Movie *The Wizard of Oz*

Cox, Stephen. *The Munchkins Remember: The Wizard of Oz and Beyond*.
    New York: E.P. Dutton, 1989.

Finch, Christopher. *Rainbow* [a biography of Judy Garland]. New York:
    Grosset & Dunlap: 1975.

Fricke, John, Jay Scarfone, and William Stillman. *The Wizard of Oz:
    The Official 50th Anniversary Pictorial History*. New York: Warner
    Books, 1989.

Harmetz, Aljean. *The Making of THE WIZARD OF OZ*. New York:
    Alfred A. Knopf, 1981, 1977.

The Wizard of Oz: The Screenplay, by Noel Langley, Florence Ryerson,
    and Edgar Allan Wolf. Edited and with an introduction by Michael
    Patrick Hearn. New York: Dell Publishing Group, 1989.

Index

Acknowledgments

The photos and illustrations in this text appear courtesy of: pp. 1, 40 (top), 102, Michael Gessell; pp. 2, 11, 12 (both), 18, 20, 24, 28 (top), 45 (right), 50, 52 (left), 54 (both), 60 (both), 62 (top and bottom), 66, 74 (right), 103, 104, 109, L. Frank Baum Papers/The George Arents Research Library for Special Collections at Syracuse University; p. 8, Chicago Historical Society; pp. 13, 48, 51, 57, 58, 126 (bottom), Patricia Drentea/The Kerlan Collection, University of Minnesota Libraries; pp. 15, 22, 28 (bottom), 97, Robert A. Baum; p. 19 (left), David Greene; 19 (right), American Antiquarian Society; p. 23, Town of Manlius (N.Y.) Historian's Office; pp. 26, 35, 74 (left), 125, *The Baum Bugle;* pp. 33 (both), 39 (top), 40 (bottom), 52 (right), 111, 114, L. Frank Baum Collection/Alexander Mitchell Library; p. 34, Smithsonian Institution National Anthropological Archives, Bureau of American Ethnology Collection; p. 38, Rose Collection, Western History Collections, University of Oklahoma Library; pp. 45 (left), 112, Library of Congress; p. 46, Maxfield Parrish/*Mother Goose in Prose*; p. 49, L. Frank Baum Collection, Clifton Waller Barrett Library, Manuscripts Division, University of Virginia Library; pp. 62 (middle), 65, 67, Theatre Collection, New York Public Library, Astor, Lenox & Tilden Foundation; p. 75, Independent Picture Collection; p. 78, San Diego Historical Society, TICOR Collection; pp. 81 (left), 93, Reilly & Britton Co.; pp. 85, 88, Patricia Drentea/University of Minnesota Libraries, photograph by L. Frank Baum; p. 106, Security Pacific Photograph Collection/Los Angeles Public Library; p. 122, John Fricke; p. 126 (top), Patricia Drentea/Kerlan Collection, University of Minnesota Libraries, courtesy of General Foods Corporate Archives; p. 128 (both), © 1939 Turner Entertainment Co., © Ren. 1966 Metro-Goldwyn Mayer Inc. All rights reserved; pp. 130, 136, Jim Simondet; p. 131, NBC, photo by Gary Null. Maps on pages 30 and 89 by Laura Westlund. Artwork by W. W. Denslow on pp. 27, 59, 61 from *The Wonderful Wizard of Oz*. Artwork by John R. Neill on pp. 2, 3, 4, 6, 9, 16, 17, 39, 41, 68, 69, 73, 76, 93 (right), 94, 95, 98, 99, 107, 113, 115, 117, 121, 123, 132, 133, 136 from the Oz series. Artwork by E. A. Nelson on pp. 77, 81 (right), 82, 83, 91, 119 from the Aunt Jane's Nieces series.

The quoted passages in this book are reprinted from:
Reprinted by courtesy of the Baum Family and the Baum Trust: pp. 66-67, Baum, Frank Joslyn, Letter to Russell P. MacFall (October 2, 1956), L. Frank Baum Papers/The George Arents Research Library for Special Collections at Syracuse University. / p. 118, Baum, L. Frank, Letter to Frank Joslyn Baum (September 2, 1918), L. Frank Baum Papers/The George Arents Research Library for Special Collections at Syracuse University. / p. 55, ———, Letter to Dr. Henry Clay Baum (April 8, 1900), The Arents Collections, New York Public Library, Astor, Lenox and Tilden Foundations. / p. 100, ———, Letter to Dr. A. E. Rumely (June 5, 1911), Lilly Library, Indiana University. / p. 120, ———, *The Magic of Oz*. Chicago: Reilly & Lee, 1919. / pp. 119, 119-120, ——— [Edith Van Dyne, pseud.], *Aunt Jane's Nieces in the Red Cross*. Chicago: Reilly & Britton, 1918 ed.

From works by L. Frank Baum: p. 91, [Edith Van Dyne, pseud.], *Aunt Jane's Nieces Abroad.* Chicago: Reilly & Britton, 1906. / p. 108, [Edith Van Dyne, pseud.], *Aunt Jane's Nieces Out West.* Chicago: The Reilly & Britton Co., 1914. / p. 47, *By the Candelabra's Glare*. Chicago: Privately printed, 1899. / p. 132, *Dorothy and the Wizard in Oz*. Chicago: The Reilly & Britton Co., 1908. / p. 101, *The Emerald City of Oz*. Chicago: The Reilly & Britton Co., 1910. / p. 55, *Father Goose, His Book*. Chicago: George M. Hill Co., 1899. / p. 73, *The Marvelous Land of Oz*. Chicago: The Reilly & Britton Co., 1904. / p. 105, Letter to S. C. Britton (January 23, 1912). / p. 111, Letter to Maud Gage Baum (October 12, 1914). / pp. 56, 58, *The New Wizard of Oz*. Indianapolis: The Bobbs-Merrill Company, 1903, 1899.

Quotations from *The Baum Bugle*, copyright © 1965-1987, are reproduced with the permission of the International Wizard of Oz Club, Box 95, Kinderhook, Illinois 62345. / pp. 42, 43, 55, 55-56, Baum, Harry Neal, "My Father was 'The Wizard of Oz'," Memories and Anecdotes of a Famous Father," *The Baum Bugle* 29, no. 2 (Autumn 1985). Copyright © 1985 by Brenda Baum Turner. Continued in 29, no. 3 (Winter 1985). / pp. 51-52, Baum, Harry Neal, "Santa Claus at the Baums'," *The Best of the Baum Bugle, 1965-1966.* / p. 95, Baum, L. Frank, "Unknown Poem of L. Frank

Baum," *The Baum Bugle* 25, no. 2 (Summer 1981). / pp. 55, 121, Baum, Maud Gage, "Dear Sergeant Snow, Maud Baum's Correspondence with Jack Snow," *The Baum Bugle* 26, no. 3 (Winter 1982). Continued in 27, no. 1 (Spring 1983). / pp. 43-44, 63, Baum, Robert Stanton, "The Autobiography of Robert Stanton Baum," *The Baum Bugle* (Christmas 1970). Continued in (Spring 1971). / pp. 96, 96-97, Fricke, John, "Romola," *The Baum Bugle* 31, no. 2 (Autumn 1987). / pp. 32, 35, Gage, Matilda J., "The Dakota Days of L. Frank Baum, Part I and II," *The Best of the Baum Bugle, 1965-1966.* / p. 80, Haff, James E., "Bibliographia Pseudonymiana: Edith Van Dyne: The 'Aunt Jane's Nieces' Series," *The Baum Bugle* 21, no. 1 (Spring 1977). / p. 126, Otto, Frederick E. and Martha Liehe, "Members' Memories of the Jell-O Show," *The Baum Bugle* 30, no. 3 (Winter 1986). / pp. 74-75, 124, "Oz Under Scrutiny: Early Reviews of The Marvelous Land of Oz," *The Baum Bugle* 23, no. 1 (Spring 1979). / p. 31, Roesch, Dr. Sally, "Matilda Jewell Gage 1886-1986," *The Baum Bugle* 30, no. 1 (Spring 1986). Copyright © 1986 by Dr. Sally Roesch Wagner. / pp. 46, 52, 92, 102, 123, Wagner, Sally Roesch, "Dorothy Gage and Dorothy Gale," *The Baum Bugle* 28, no. 2 (Autumn 1984). ·

Other sources: pp 31-32, *The Aberdeen Daily News*, 1888./ pp. 36, 37, 38, *The Aberdeen Saturday Pioneer* (December 13, 1890); also (December 27, 1890); also (January 3, 1891)./ pp. 20, 39, 45, 53, Reprinted with permission of *American Heritage* 16, no. 1 (December 1964), from "The Father of the Wizard of Oz" by Daniel P. Mannix. Copyright © 1964 by American Heritage, a division of Forbes, Inc. / p. 133, Reprinted with permission of the American Library Association, from *American Library Association Bulletin* (October 1957), "Ralph Ulveling on Freedom of Information" by Ralph Ulveling. / pp. 21, 25, 27, 29, 44, MacFall, Russell P. and Frank Joslyn Baum. *To Please a Child: A Biography of L. Frank Baum Royal Historian of Oz.* Chicago: Reilly & Lee, 1961. / pp. 49, 103, Baum, Harry Neal, "How My Father Wrote the Oz Books," *American Book Collector* (December 1962). / pp. 83-90, Baum, Maud Gage. *In Other Lands Than Ours: A Series of Letters from Abroad.* Chicago: Privately printed, 1907. Delmar, New York: Scholars' Facsimiles & Reprints, 1983. / p. 9, Bowden, Ramona B., "A File Drawer Caught His Eye," *Syracuse Post-Standard* (December 20, 1978). / p. 116, [Buffalo, N.Y.] *Express* (November 5, 1916). / p. 10, Campbell, Mary, interview with L. Frank Baum. *Milwaukee Sentinel*, 1900. / p. 115, *The Chicago Tribune*, book review (December 19, 1915). Copyrighted, Dec. 19, 1915 Chicago Tribune Company, all rights reserved, used with permission. / p. 135, "45 Years of 'The Wizard'," *Collier's* (February 9, 1946). / pp. 129-130, *L. Frank Baum: The Wonderful Wizard of Oz: An Exhibition of His Published Writings, in Commemmoration of the Centenary of His Birth, May 15, 1856*, Rare Book and Manuscript Library, Columbia University (May 1956), Addenda. Used with permission. / pp. 44, 125, Greene, David L. and Dick Martin. *The Oz Scrapbook.* New York: Random House, 1977. Copyright © 1977 David L. Greene and Dick Martin. / p. 37, Haas, Joseph, "The Wonderful Writer of Oz," *The* [Chicago] *Daily News* Panorama (April 17, 1965). / p. 127, Hearn, Michael Patrick. From *The Wizard of Oz: The Screenplay* by Noel Langley, Florence Ryerson & Edgar Allen Woolf. Edited with an Introduction by Michael Patrick Hearn. New York: Dell Publishing Group, Inc., 1989. Used with permission. / p. 67, Hearn, Michael Patrick. *The Annotated Wizard of Oz* by L. Frank Baum. Introduction, Notes, and Bibliography by Michael Patrick Hearn. New York: Clarkson Potter, 1973. Copyright © 1973 by Michael Patrick Hearn. Used with permission. / p. 48, *The Home Magazine*, 1899. / p. 67, Leslie, Amy, "The Wizard of Oz," *The* [Chicago] *Daily News* (June 17, 1902). / pp. 64-65, Maier, Max, Letter to Russell P. MacFall (October 27, 1956). L. Frank Baum Papers/ The George Arents Research Library for Special Collections at Syracuse University. / p. 129, Maloney, Russell, "The Wizard of Oz," *The New Yorker* (August 19, 1939). / p. 25, *New York Mirror* theater reviews (June 24, 1882). / p. 59, *The New York Times* book reviews (1900). Copyright © 1900 by The New York Times Company. Reprinted by permission. / pp. 14, 72-73, 78, (Philadelphia) *North American*, interview with L. Frank Baum (October 3, 1904). / p. 101, *The* [Portland, Ore.] *Telegram*, book review (October 22, 1910). / p. 118, Reprinted from page 1300 of the October 19, 1918 issue of *Publishers Weekly*, published by the R.R. Bowker Company. Copyright © 1918 by the R.R. Bowker Company. / p. 24, Rivette, Barbara S., *Fayetteville's First Woman Voter — Matilda Joslyn Gage.* Manlius, New York: League of Women Voters, 1970. Copyright © 1970 by Barbara S. Rivette. / p. 79, Tietjens, Eunice, *The World at My Shoulder.* New York: Macmillan, 1938. Used by permission of Marshall Head. / pp. 66, 121, 134, widely seen.